*Neighbor Girl*

# *Neighbor Girl*

RALPH COURSOLLE

Copyright 1999 by Ralph Coursolle
ISBN: 0-9666819-1-6

All rights reserved, including the right to reproduce this book in or any portion thereof in any form whatsoever.

First Printing 1999

Front cover photography courtesy of and copyright by Mitchelss Lee Photography, Roseville, CA
Cover design copyright by Tamara Dever, TLC Graphics, Folsom, CA

I lovingly dedicate this book to my late wife, Marie, whose love and devotion were the inspiration for the words to this book and to my five children; Jim, Judy, Jeannie, Jerry and Jaci who continue to bless me.

*Neighbor Girl*

## Chapter 1

THE BEDSIDE ALARM CLOCK chimed six times before it awakened Ben Smith. He pushed the covers off and stepped out with a sudden awareness that this was the day for his trip to the Twin Cities. His few aches and pains were due to his age and perhaps the care giving years before his wife had passed away. A warm shower and anti-inflammatory pill followed by banana and cereal breakfast would help. He planned on picking up Julie Evans, his neighbor girl, in a couple of hours. She would drive with him to St. Paul where he had been selected by his former law school to act as a judge of students participating in a moot court case on espionage.

Before retirement Ben Smith had been a trial lawyer in Minneapolis after World War II. After retirement and a diagnosis that his wife had Alzheimer's disease, he moved to Milaca. He purchased a small two-bedroom house whose dark-stained log siding was a colorful contrast to the spacious green lawn and evergreen trees. Shortly after they moved into their home, Ben noticed a young couple with a baby move into the white house with black shutters across the street. He developed an acquaintance with the young couple, watching the mother frequently play with her daughter in their front yard. After a few years he became aware of the young husband's absence. Neighbors said he was gone.

The acquaintance between Ben and his neighbor girl grew with the help of the child named Chrissy, now five years old, who frequently would shout, "Hi, Ben" when he was out in his yard. Because they had been friendly neighbors for the past five years, he thought about asking Julie to help him drive to the Cities. He phoned her.

"Julie, I've been asked to be a judge at a seminar at my law school in St. Paul. I feel a little insecure about doing all the driving to and from the Cities. Could you go with me and help me in the driving?"

"When will it be, Ben?"

"Two weeks from today."

"How long will we be gone? I'll have to get a sitter for Chrissy."

"We'll leave in the morning and be back the same day by supper time. I'll be happy to pay you for helping me and also for Chrissy's sitter."

"Okay, Ben. What should I wear?"

"It's nothing fancy. Just wear casual clothes."

"I'll help you but I can't drive within the Cities. I can drive until we get on the outskirts of St. Paul."

"I'll take over driving when we get near St. Paul."

"Will we be alone?"

"Yes. I'll phone you the day before. We'll leave early."

Ben had developed a fondness for his neighbor girl. Maybe it was her obvious need for companionship, or perhaps her beauty and friendliness that aroused the fondness. She was a petite brunette with hazel eyes. Her curvaceous build, pleasant smile and congeniality were attractive to Ben. Julie's own father had disappeared but her mother lived in Milaca. Perhaps he could help solve the father problem for Julie who seemed willing to relate many of her personal problems to him. He wondered, however, why she asked him if they would be alone. Did she think he had other than friendly motives for the attention he gave to her?

He turned off the alarm, put on his robe and headed for the bathroom shower. While soaping himself he began singing. How had two weeks gone by so swiftly?

The tune had always been his favorite one about Marie and Gertrude. His wife's first and second names were Marie and Gertrude. She didn't care for the name Gertrude. He recalled addressing her as Gert a couple of times in kidding. She was gone now. He was alone, but he enjoyed visiting and talking with Julie and Chrissy. Dressed and fed, he went to his car. He drove across the street to Julie's, got out and walked around to open the passenger door for her. They headed south on Highway 169 from Milaca. A few miles out of town he stopped the car.

"Why are we stopping in this park?"

"So we can change drivers," Ben answered casually.

They changed positions, and Julie drove until they got to Rogers, a small community through which freeway I-94 passed on the way into the Twin Cities. Ben took over the driving to and through the Cities to the law school.

Upon arrival at the school, they walked into the room that had been set up as a court room. Ben suggested to Julie that she stay with him and watch the proceedings so she sat down in the back of the room. Julie observed a couple of other lawyers join Ben in discussion before the start of the proceedings. A young lawyer in his late twenties, Brad Owens, would act as a judge with Ben. He looked at Julie as she walked to the rear of the improvised court in a classroom. He noticed that she looked his way after she sat down. Each time Julie looked toward Brad she became aware he was looking at her. Throughout the activities Ben's attention was continuously drawn to the eye contacts between Julie and the young lawyer. He continued to watch them during the rest of the seminar. As Ben and Julie rode back to Milaca, he wondered, had Julie and the young lawyer become attracted to each other? What did the continuous eye contacts between them mean?

Later in the week Ben had his lunch at the cafe in Milaca where Julie worked as a waitress. He was accompanied by an acquaintance in the community. Ben told the story of his trip to the law school seminar with Julie, pointing her out to his lunch partner. The cafe seated about 40 people in booths along the north wall and a number of tables for four in the center. Stools lined a counter at the back. Shingle-covered overhangs, wall lamps and ceiling fans completed its decor. Ben explained how the young lawyer and Julie watched one another during the seminar. His acquaintance appeared interested in the story. His friend turned to Ben.

"It sounds like you had a good trip."

"Yes, it went well."

"I'll bet you wondered about the lady and young lawyer watching each other."

"It did intrigue me. I sensed there was an attraction between them."

"Did she meet the young lawyer?"

"I forgot to introduce them and he was absent from the room when we left to go home."

"You've known the neighbor for some time?"

"Yes. I think it's been about five years."

"What's she like?"

"She seems quite nice. She lives across the street with her young daughter. She obviously felt there was a mistake in her young marriage. She seems a little skeptical and more than a bit cautious in her responses."

"Is she from here?"

"She was born here in Milaca and went to school

here. Her mother and a younger sister live in the vicinity of Milaca. I think this town is her roots and probably always will be. She hasn't seen her father for some time, but I suppose that's a whole other story."

## Chapter 2

Brad Owens practiced law in Minneapolis. Six years had elapsed since he graduated. He had been a good student and had played football on the University team in his pre-law years. He was born on the outskirts of Minneapolis and reared in one of its western suburbs. His parents and a brother still lived in the homestead but he had chosen to live alone in his bachelor apartment near Loring Park for the past three years. His friend and fellow lawyer, John Larimore, kidded him about always being a bachelor.

"With your six-foot height and athletic build, tan complexion and looks, some gal should have grabbed you by now."

Brad generally responded that he had plenty of time and for now he was more interested in the law practice.

Brad was going full steam ahead in his law practice when he saw this girl with Ben Smith at the law school seminar. He could not keep his eyes off her, but he missed getting her name and she and Ben Smith left during Brad's absence from the room. He wanted to see her again, but how? Would he ever see her again? Should he bother the school to get Ben Smith's number and phone him for her address and phone number?

The image of the girl was floating through Brad's mind as he opened his law office door. The image disappeared for a second or two while he observed his office surroundings. His private office had a four-by-eight foot glass topped desk and high back leather chair, with a library table at right angles to his desk. He glanced at the legal certificates on the walls of the office but the glance stopped when he again saw the image of the girl who had been at the legal seminar the previous day. What was the attraction? She was beautiful, but why this girl out of all the women he had seen before her?

"I've got to meet her," he said aloud to himself. He tried to concentrate on the file he had placed in front of him, but the image of the girl appeared again.

Brad was stunned by the thoughts he was having of this woman. He could still see her sitting in back of the moot court room, obviously watching him. Again he wondered who she was. How did she happen to be with that older man? Were his thoughts genuine or a fantasy? He knew he never had thoughts like this about any other girl.

John Larimore, a legal associate, knocked on Brad's office door, then walked in and sat down in one of the chairs facing the large office desk. He had a desk calendar in his left hand and a pen in the other.

"Hey, buddy. You look dazed. Somethin' the matter?"
"No, not really."
"Got a minute to talk?"
"For you, John, always. What's up?"
"Shouldn't we drive up to Duluth soon to look at the facilities for the summer convention?"
"Good idea. When do you think we should make the drive?"
"How about this coming Saturday?"
"Okay with me. I'll drive."

Brad sat back in his chair and crossed his legs to listen to John. They had been working together for some time on the Minnesota Bar Association plans for the legal convention the following summer in Duluth. John felt it was time to start moving on the plans by going to Duluth to observe and arrange for the location of seminar rooms and other matters for the convention.

John marked the date for the coming Saturday on his pocket calendar.

"How do you want to get there, on the freeway?"

Brad moved his chair closer to his desk.

"Why don't we drive up 169 and have lunch on the way?"

John agreed and as he stood up to leave, remarked,

"We can discuss our plans for the summer bar convention on the way up."

Perhaps, Brad thought, he would tell John about Julie on the way up to Duluth.

On Saturday morning Brad picked up John at his home. It was a beautiful, Minnesota fall day, a season of changing colors, some bright yellow and red, dazzling in appearance under the morning sun. The panorama was like a painted mural along the highway. The coloring of the oak and maple was offset at times with perfectly shaped evergreens that stood as sentinels over the other trees. Brad and John chatted about this beautiful picture as they drove north along the highway. Brad turned to John.

"When you asked me if I had a girlfriend yesterday I told myself I would tell you today. I saw a girl at a law school seminar a while back and I just can't get her out of my mind."

Brad proceeded to explain that he had not met her because she and the man she was with left the seminar while he was absent from the room.

"Boy, what I wouldn't give to see her again."

"You actually fell for a girl you just saw and don't know or haven't even met?"

"I think so, John."

"Well, well. Isn't this an historical event," was John's rather gleeful response.

Late into the morning the car approached Milaca in the midst of a discussion on the plans for the convention. John mentioned that there was a cafe in the town which had good food. They drove down the main street until they saw the Pinewood Cafe sign. The two men walked into the cafe and looked for a table. Brad stopped suddenly, prompting John to quiz him.

"What's the matter with you?"

"There! There!" mumbled Brad a bit excitedly. "That's her."

"That's who?"

"Over there at the counter next to the kitchen. The woman I saw at the law school seminar."

"Hold on. Are you sure she's the same woman?"

"I know it's her."

Brad pointed to a booth. They were able to see the girl standing at the serving counter, her back, braided dark hair down it, to them. The young woman picked up plates of food and carried them to one of the tables to be served. She looked up and spotted Brad. She thought she knew him. With a surprised look, she walked slowly toward the booth.

"Would you like menus?"

Brad swallowed hard a couple of times before he said, "It's you."

"Yup, it's me."

"What are you doing here?"

"I work here; well, I live here in Milaca and this is where I work."

She wiped off the table then went to get menus and utensils. As she walked away, Brad admired her figure. Intuitively, he knew this was the person he had always wanted, the woman of his dreams. He said to himself,

"The search is over." He experienced an excitement and stirring he never had felt before.

The men both ordered a club house sandwich which Brad said tasted better than any sandwich he had eaten before. The waitress smiled while she walked about the cafe. Occasionally she would catch Brad's eye. She could feel him watching her as she went about her duties. Her body tingled as she thought about the happiness the sight of him brought her. She reminisced about her trip to the law school with Ben and she wondered if Ben knew about Brad. She knew she wanted to see this person again and hoped he would say something that would bring about another meeting between them. Brad looked up at John, "I never expected to see this young woman again. What made us decide to stop at this cafe?"

"It's fate, Brad. Think about it. It's fate that sometimes brings people together, ya know?"

Julie stopped again at their booth.

"We have wonderful chocolate cream pie."

"Sounds great. Make it two."

When Julie returned with the pie, Brad asked her how she knew Ben Smith. Brad said he recalled that Ben mentioned that he was from Milaca.

"Yes, I know Ben. He's my neighbor."

"Have you known him long?"

"I guess it's been about five years. He's a wonderful neighbor."

"I think he told me at the seminar that he was retired."

"Uh, huh. He had a law practice in Minneapolis but when his wife got Alzheimer's they moved up here. She passed away a couple of years ago."

Julie glanced at other patrons waiting to be served, put the check on the table and turned to walk away.

"Do you mind if I phone you?" whispered Brad almost breathlessly.

"I'd like that." She scribbled her number on the check and left the booth. As they walked to the car after paying the cashier, Brad turned to John.

"I can't believe it's her!"

"She's pretty. She sure has gotten your attention. Uhhh, maybe you aren't going to be a bachelor after all."

"I'd like to ask her to go on the spring Caribbean cruise legal seminar with me."

"But you don't even know her."

"Well, okay. So maybe we'll have to try a couple of dates first."

"Good luck, Buddy, you need a woman in your life. I hope it works out for you."

They headed to Lake Mille Lacs. The sun glistened as it reflected off the calm, blue waters. They talked about the various resorts along the lake with the beauty of elm and oak trees' colors of red and yellow. Thirty miles further would bring them to Thompson Hill with the breathtaking view of Lake Superior and its harbor. From the top of the hill they could see the vast, almost endless, stretch of the lake, the draw bridge and the ore boats moving about the harbor.

The Duluth Convention Center overlooked Lake Superior. It had an atrium, various meeting rooms, and a large auditorium. After being given a tour of the facilities by the manager of the convention center, they headed for their car to drive back to the Twin Cities. Brad seemed quieter than usual as they drove along the highway. He reviewed his lunch at the Pinewood Cafe in Milaca where he saw Julie. She had been on his mind since the legal seminar. Now that he had seen her again, he was certain that she was the woman he wanted to ask to go with him on the spring Caribbean Cruise legal seminar. He again had the feeling that she was the girl of his dreams.

Brad returned to his apartment that afternoon in time to go jogging around part of Lake Calhoun. He wove his over six-foot frame between the bicycles along the cart path. He lifted his broad chest to the breeze as he jogged at a careful pace. His thoughts again returned to the girl he had just seen at noon in the Milaca Cafe. He interrupted his jogging to sit on a bench along the cart path to get his wind and try to collect his thoughts. He closed his eyes and draped his left arm over the back rest, ensconced in thoughts of his past life with his own family, his years of studying to become a lawyer and his inner desire to find someone as a mate whom he could love. He wondered if the girl in the cafe might be trying to fulfill the same kind of dream.

## Chapter 3

JULIE HAD JUST WORKED the morning shift at the Pinewood Cafe in Milaca. She looked forward to visiting with Carol Dahl, her long time friend with whom she became acquainted in high school. Carol, her strawberry hair and freckled skin, a few inches taller than Julie but also of slender build, was quite a contrast to Julie with her dark hair and tanned skin. Julie and Carol saw each other almost daily. This afternoon would be no exception. Carol would visit Julie and together they would sit in Julie's yard and catch up with each others' lives. Chrissy, Julie's daughter, was a typical five-year old and would play in the yard while her mother and Carol visited. Chrissy had her mother's coloring and facial features. A vibrant child, she often became the center of attention and conversation when Julie and Carol visited.

Chrissy, scheduled to enter Kindergarten the following year, could recite the alphabet and knew her arithmetic tables to number nine. Julie often mentioned to Carol how badly she hoped Chrissy would go to college. Both Carol and Julie had experienced much the same type of marital problems as a result of marriages which took place shortly after high school graduation. The only real difference between them was that Carol did not have a child. The close friendship which started in high school still existed, and was stronger than ever.

Julie left the cafe after finishing the morning and noon waitress shift. On her way home, she stopped at the daycare for Chrissy, then drove home to the northeast end of Milaca. She parked in the dirt driveway, helped Chrissy from the car, let Chrissy in the house, then walked along the side of the house to view the colorful flowers before ending up near the garden planted in the back yard. She took pride in the garden she had planted in the spring, nurturing it so she could now pick vegetables for a meal. After picking some green beans and pulling a tomato off a vine, she walked into the house to find Chrissy watching TV. Julie knelt down by Chrissy.

"Have a good day, honey?"

"Uh, huh."

"Can you tell me some of the things you did?"

"We used big cards with letters on them."

"You mean alphabet cards?"

"Uh, huh."

"So you learned some more about letters today, huh?"

"Can you tell me how which ones you learned?"

"A, B, C, D, E, and F."

"That's real good, Chrissy. Tomorrow's my day off. Want to walk up town and I can tell you about some of the buildings and the old train depot?"

"That'd be fun, Mom."

The next day Julie dressed in a light blouse, slacks and tennis shoes. Good for a walk, she thought. She dressed Chrissy in light clothes also since it was a warm, autumn day. The grass was still green though the leaves were turning colors. As they left the house together, they walked holding hands, headed toward downtown Milaca.

When they reached the center of town, they ambled toward the railroad depot which had become a historical center. The train no longer carried passenger traffic but freight and coal cars were still hauled over the rails. The old depot walls were filled with photographs and pictures depicting the past era of the community. Logging had been a predominant industry of the community in the early 20th century with farming an economic mainstay for the inhabitants of the surrounding land. Julie smiled as she explained the mementos on the walls to Chrissy. She felt that Chrissy was old enough, and bright enough, to understand her explanations.

After leaving the historical center, they walked toward the town's only signal light at the main intersection that swayed on wires from opposite poles. They sauntered past glass fronts of the shops and other businesses along the street. As Julie peered in the plate glass windows and saw her own reflection, a mental picture of the young lawyer suddenly appeared. Thoughts began to take form. She was in her hometown where she had been born and reared. She had always wanted to live here. She had no desire to head for the big cities or to live in them. She enjoyed a trip to the Cities, if necessary, but she was content to stay in Milaca.

Julie led Chrissy into the nearest drugstore to get some shampoo and nail polish, warning Chrissy not to touch anything on the shelves. On their way home, they made a game of kicking loose stones along the sidewalk which rattled as they hit the edges of the cement slabs of sidewalk. Again, her thoughts turned unexpectedly to Brad. She realized she was anxious to see him again.

Once Julie and Chrissy returned from their walk, Julie phoned Carol.

"Why don't you drop over for a while?"

"I'll be right over."

Carol's car pulled up in Julie's driveway within the next fifteen minutes. They took out a couple of folding chairs and sat down under the stalwart oak trees which shaded them from the bright sunny day with its high temperatures and humidity. Chrissy stomped over to her swing set to amuse herself.

"Look Mom! I can swing high."

"Not too high, Chrissy," as she turned to Carol.

"What's new, girl?"

"Same old grind. Work late nights and sleep part of the morning."

"Anything new with you, Julie?"

"Not really. Still working the same shift at the Pinewood. But I'm trying to get the assistant manager position."

"What are you doing, besides waiting on people in the cafe, that's gonna help the cause?"

"This is between you and me. I try to work a little harder than the rest and make suggestions to the manager about the preparation of the food and its layout on the plates."

"No offense, Jules, but how many ways are there to serve a hamburger, if you know what I mean."

"I think you can arrange the food so as to make it more appetizing."

"So, what does the manager say to all of this?"

"So far he's been pretty open to my ideas and actually seems grateful."

"Really? Have you suggested other things?"

"I told him just the other day that I thought we could be more attentive to our patrons by keeping the water glasses and coffee cups filled without being asked."

"What'd he say?"

"Well, really, what could he say? He doesn't like it

when patrons call over to a waitress to bring more water or coffee."

"Well, go girl!"

"I have some lemonade in the house. Want some?"

"Sounds delicious."

Julie walked toward her kitchen door then whirled around quickly.

"Carol, I have some other ideas I can't wait to tell you about."

Sitting back in her lawn chair after handing Carol and Chrissy some lemonade, Julie turned to Carol again.

"You know, Carol. I've always wanted to try and fulfill a crazy daydream I've had."

"What's that?"

"I want to get somewhere, be somebody, do something."

"But you already have a good job and good ideas about improving it."

"But this has been a daydream I've had for some time. Someday, soon, I want to try to fulfill it."

"Just what it is you plan to do?"

"Well, I finished well above average in a typing course in high school and I can still type with some speed and accuracy."

"Yes, I remember. . . ." her voice trailed off as if in reminiscing. With genuine interest now, she asked,

"What exactly are you talking about?"

"This is between us—but I would like to build an antique business."

"Like a garage sale?"

"No, Carol, the real thing. You know, buying and selling antiques."

"Where would you get them?"

"I'd attend farm auctions, garage sales and places where antiques are bought and sold. At least, that's where I'd start, I think."

"But where would you get that kind of money to buy them?"

"Promise not to tell anyone?"

Carol shifted in her chair. "I swear."

Julie leaned over toward Carol. "I've already started saving a little each week from my earnings and tips."

"How much do you think you'd need to start buying and how would you sell them?"

"I'd probably need at least a thousand dollars. 'Course, I'd have to find out the best means of selling the antiques once I found them."

Carol's interest in Julie's dream grew as they chatted.

"Wow, Julie, it sounds like a terrific idea. You're brilliant."

"No, not really. It's just that I want to get somewhere and have something that I wanted to do myself."

"Got a place for me in this plan?"

"Trust me, I've been thinking about that too."

Chrissy jumped from the swing and made her way over to the two.

"I've got to go into the house, Mom."

Julie helped Chrissy make her way to the bathroom. Carol followed them into the house and planted herself on the sofa in the living room. Julie joined her momentarily and they continued their conversation.

"But the buy and sell ideas. What made you come up with that idea?"

"I went to the library in town and started skimming through magazines and feature articles about antiques. Everything just sort of fell into place, really."

Chrissy called from the bathroom for assistance. When Julie and Chrissy returned, Chrissy rhythmically but quietly began to rock in her small red rocking chair while the women picked up the conversation again as if there had been no break or lapse in it.

"But isn't it going to interfere with your waitress job?"

"I don't plan to start anything until I've saved enough money and hopefully I'll make enough at selling that I can eventually afford to quick my job at the cafe."

"So you really do plan to follow the daydream?"

"Yes, at the right time. It may not be tomorrow or even next year, but I will do it. But you must promise Carol—not a word to anyone."

"I promise," as she headed for the door. "I've gotta run some errands yet. Best be on my way."

She stepped outside after thanking Julie and saying good-bye to Chrissy. The rays of sun had bent a little in the west casting their light over part of the green grass not shaded by the great oak trees. Carol waved good-bye to Julie and Chrissy until another day.

Julie thought about Ben whom she and her former husband met when they moved across from the retired lawyer. There was some reluctance on her part to further the acquaintance; she gave it a lot of thought. He was white-haired, quite a bit older than she but, as they visited, she became more comfortable with him. She sometimes wondered if his intentions were only neighborly when she saw him standing in his lawn watching her while she was sunbathing in her yard. She realized after a while that what his interest in her were for her and Chrissy's benefit and she confided in him more and more about matters of a personal nature. She told Ben about her relatives, her divorce, her loneliness and difficulties with some men she had dated. They agreed to have lunch together about once a month and to go shopping together in a larger town nearby.

## Chapter 4

As the birds left their nests for the south and the chilling autumn nights signaled that winter was on its way, Brad thought it was about time to phone Julie and ask her if she would mind his driving up to visit her. Brad found himself daydreaming about her often. Sometimes he envisioned her standing before him with her arms open. Each moment of day-dreaming only enhanced his desire to take her in his arms and tell her his feelings about her. He firmly resolved, however, that he shouldn't do that on his first visit. It was the end of October when Julie answered the phone and the caller identified himself as Brad Owens.

"Hi, Julie. I saw you not too long ago at the Pinewood Cafe. Remember me?"

"Yes, of course. You were also at the law school seminar, right?"

"That's right, Julie. I'd like to visit you if that would be all right?"

"That'd be fine. About when are you coming?"

"How's Saturday at 4:00 in the afternoon?"

Julie felt excited. "You have my address?"

"Yes, I can find you."

Brad hung up the phone, sat back in his office chair with his hands clasped behind his neck. He felt exhilarated. He felt an eagerness to climb a tall mountain although he knew nothing about mountain climbing.

Saturday arrived. Brad felt a peculiar excitement as he walked up to Julie's door. She appeared in the doorway wearing a black skirt and white low-neckline blouse. He thought she looked more beautiful than when he had seen her at the cafe or the law school. He was about to tell her she was pretty when he collected himself.

"It's great to see you."

She smiled, "Please come in."

He couldn't believe how nervous he felt. All he could think of to say was "Thanks."

As she stepped back, Brad crossed the threshold and sat down opposite the sofa. He felt a bit shaky as he lowered his brief case with Caribbean cruise plans in it to the floor beside his chair.

"Was it a nice drive up here?"

"Yes. Had to do some work at my office before I left, otherwise I would have gotten an early start."

Brad still felt a little fidgety as he crossed and uncrossed his legs. He wondered if it was too soon to talk about the Caribbean Cruise seminar. He waited for her to say something as he sneaked a look around the living room.

"Would you like a soda, lemonade, beer. . . ?" Julie asked, standing up from the sofa. "Any trouble finding my house?"

"A Coke would be nice, if you have it. No, I didn't have any trouble. Your directions were perfect."

Julie walked out to the kitchen to get a cola. " She's pretty," Brad thought. He told her that he thought her house was charming. He perspired some, reached for his handkerchief and wiped his brow. As he began to feel more comfortable, the perspiration seemed to stop. Julie was glad she was having a visit from a good-looking young man. He looked tanned too—perhaps over six feet in height, quite muscular, with strong hands. His hair was dark but she noticed his eyes were blue.

"You have a nice home," as he reached down beside his chair to touch his briefcase. He wondered how he would approach Julie about the cruise seminar. He didn't want to start talking about it until he felt more at ease.

"That's quite a bright yellow kitchen you've got there."

"Would you like to see the rest of the house?"

"Sure."

"The kitchen isn't very large but it's big enough for my daughter Chrissy and me."

"You have a breakfast nook. How quaint. The rest seems quite modern."

"We like the nook. In fact we eat all of our meals there. I still don't have a dishwasher so we do our dishes the good, old-fashioned way" she said with a bit of a grin.

"I like the yellow and the wallpapering around the top of the kitchen walls. Do it yourself?"

"No, actually the kitchen was decorated that way when I bought the house. C'mon. I'll show you the rest."

Brad followed her toward the bedrooms, where she pointed out that the one to the right was hers. There was a bathroom and then her daughter Chrissy's bedroom beyond the bathroom.

"It's really quite nice. When did you move here?"

"About five years ago."

"You and your daughter live alone?"

"Uh, huh."

Brad didn't feel he should be too inquisitive. He now knew Julie and her daughter were alone and that was enough for the first visit. He would have liked to find out how she happened to be living alone with a daughter, but was reluctant to inquire. He checked her left hand. She wasn't wearing a wedding ring. Suddenly he felt a bit nervous again; he questioned telling her about the spring cruise seminar until he knew more about her past.

"Julie, I wonder if I could ask you a very personal question?"

Julie smiled, "I'll bet you want to know more about me."

Brad moved nervously in the sofa chair. He wondered if this was the way to get acquainted. He questioned mentally the propriety of even suggesting that he wanted to ask a personal question. Still he had to know something about her before he could broach the question about the spring Caribbean cruise seminar. Julie sensed his uneasiness and took it upon herself to continue the conversation.

"I'm divorced; Chrissy is at my mother's house for the afternoon."

"Then your parents live here in Milaca?"

"My mother lives here. She's remarried. I don't know where my father is."

Julie eyed Brad as her mind toyed with thoughts of the good-looking man seated opposite her in her living room.

"I like him. He seems to be somebody I might enjoy being with," she mused to herself.

Brad interrupted her daydreaming.

"I know I've only seen you twice, but it seems like I've known you for so much longer than that. What I'd like to ask you may not meet with your approval."

Julie asked him if he'd like another Coke since she

was going to get one for herself. Was she trying to make him more comfortable?

"You do know I'm a lawyer."

"I gathered as much when I saw you at the law school seminar."

"Well, a few months ago the planning committee of our State Bar Association decided to hold its spring convention on a Caribbean cruise that will last a week."

"The bar association?"

"It's an organization of lawyers used primarily for continuing education on the rules and regulations of the legal profession."

"You mentioned a Caribbean cruise. So, you lawyers go sailing, huh? To study, or have fun?"

"Well, a little of both, actually." Brad moved up to the front edge of his sofa chair. "And I'd like to have you join me on the cruise in March of next year."

Julie smiled, but almost immediately her expression registered doubt and surprise as her mind tried to answer the question. She quizzically repeated, "You're asking me to go with you on the cruise?"

Brad saw the doubt and surprise expressed by her and tried to soften the apparent impact on the young lady.

"Not to worry. There'll be a large group of lawyers and their wives. Some may have their sweethearts along, too."

Julie tried to smile again. "This is awfully sudden. Could you tell me more?"

"I know it's sudden, but you're the only woman I would want to take on the cruise. Let me explain, if I can. When I saw you at the law school seminar, I began thinking about you." He went on to explain that when he saw her again at the Pinewood Cafe that she's been on his mind often and that he was certain he wanted to take her on the cruise seminar. He knew in his heart and mind that he had fallen in love with her, but he couldn't tell her that now. So he went on to explain that the cruise would leave Florida and travel to the Caribbean islands of St. Thomas and St. Marten with stops at Nassau in the Bahamas and San Juan in Puerto Rico. The afternoons and evenings would be free for relaxation.

Julie was definitely caught off guard at the suddenness of Brad's question and wondered how she should answer him. It had been a long time since a man sat across from her that she liked. Before she could answer him he said,

"Julie, it will be a chance to get better acquainted."

Her mind was racing. She wanted to say yes, but should she be doing something like this? She stood up for a second and then sat down again, pulling her skirt down to her knees.

"Tell me more, like where would I be staying?"

"I've already checked on the cabin. The planning committee told me that the cabins available have twin separate beds, an outside veranda but one bathroom."

Julie saw her mom's car pull up into her driveway. She roused herself and went to the front door to get Chrissy, announcing to her mother she had the visitor she had mentioned earlier. Julie brought Chrissy in, helped her remove her jacket, and then brought her by the hand to meet Brad who shook her hand and told her he was happy to meet her. Chrissy smiled, then climbed up on the sofa to sit next to her mother just long enough for Julie to explain that Chrissy was five years old and would start kindergarten. Chrissy sauntered off to her room to play with her dolls.

"So, about the cabin—what is it like?"

Brad understood that what she was really asking for was a more specific description of the sleeping arrangements.

"Julie, the cabin will have separate twin beds, each against a cabin wall alone with a chest of drawers or vanity in between them. There is a veranda where he can sit and visit and a single bathroom with shower."

Julie was a little surprised by the answer and asked if any of the cabins had more than one bedroom. Brad said he would talk to the planning committee again about the cabin arrangements. He planned to make another drive to the summer convention site in Duluth and asked Julie if he could visit her again.

"We could have dinner and talk about the cruise a little more, and just get to know one another better."

Julie smiled, stood up and walked about the living room.

"I'll need to give this some serious thought."

As Brad walked out the door he replied, "I know this must seem rather unusual, but you really are the only one I want to take on this cruise." Julie closed the front door then walked to the phone to call Carol and ask her friend if she would drop over to sometime that day. Julie and Carol were intimate friends, the kind of friends whose secrets they told one another. Without hesitation, Carol said she'd be right over.

Julie liked Brad, but she still wanted her friend's opinion and also her mom's. As she went to the bedroom to get Chrissy, she attempted to visualize the ship cabin Brad had described to her. She realized she'd be sleeping in the same cabin room with him.

Julie began to think aloud. "I've been making it on my own for five years now. I'm not afraid of much of anything; he seems like a person I can trust."

Carol's knock on the front door broke Julie's concentration.

"Something important, Julie?"

"Well. . . this man I saw at the law seminar and at the cafe visited me today."

"Did you like him?"

"He's good looking and really built."

"So you fell for him?"
"Sorta."
"You gonna see him again?"
"I think so. But I want to talk to you about a Caribbean cruise he wants me to go on with him."
"When?"
"Next spring. It's a cruise with legal seminars in the morning for him and afternoons and evenings for fun."
"Sounds okay to me."
"But we're going to sleep in the same cabin."
"The same bed?"
"No, no. Twin beds on opposite walls of the cabin, but the same bathroom."
"Just wear a robe."
"Carol, I know I can wear a robe. What d'ya think about sleeping in the same cabin with him?"
"Well, I suppose it could pose a problem, but knowing you, I think you can handle it okay."
"You think it's okay?"
"Well, I suppose that depends on what happens when you're together in the cabin," she said with a bit of a twinkle and a smile.
"Very funny. Seriously, you know what I've been through the last six or seven years. I can stand on my own two feet. I'll be just fine, don't ya think?"
"Go for it."
Soon the conversation twisted its way around other events happening in their hometown.

"Julie, why don't we go out a few evenings soon? We haven't had a night out in a long time."

"Got some place in mind?"

Carol suggested a night club and said she'd watch the local newspaper for announcements of any bands performing in the area. Carol left and Julie phoned her mom.

Julie answered her phone a few weeks later to hear Brad on the line.

"Julie, I'm driving up to Duluth on Saturday. How about I stop and see you on the way back? Will you have dinner with me? Let's find a place where it's quiet and we can talk."

Julie was glad to hear from him and had to admit to herself she had missed him.

"I'm supposed to work that day, but I'll get someone to cover for me."

"Great! I'll pick you up at about four o'clock. Let's take Chrissy along."

Brad had taken off his jacket and tie, opened the neck of his shirt and rolled up his sleeves before he left Duluth on Saturday afternoon. When he arrived at Julie's she noticed his hairy chest and strong forearms.

"Hunk of a man," she thought.

Brad scanned the interior of the little house as he sat down in the same chair he used before while Julie disappeared into the bedroom with Chrissy. The house was small but neat. A TV and VCR stood in one corner of the living room along with bookcase shelves of photos of friends and some knick-knacks. A framed photo of Chrissy was on the top shelf. The living room also had a sofa, two side chairs, end tables and lamps to complete the picture.

Julie and Chrissy walked out of the bedroom to be greeted by Brad.

"Well, don't you two look nice." He shook Chrissy's hand then turned to Julie to tell her she looked beautiful.

"Thanks. I know a quiet place where we can have dinner. My friend Ben told me about a place just beyond the next town where he says the food is delicious."

Julie asked if they could first drop Chrissy off at her girl friend's while they were at dinner. Brad felt relieved since he was concerned that the discussion between Julie and him perhaps should not be heard by Chrissy.

"By the way, where does he live?"

Julie motioned to the front window. "See that brown house across the street—that's his place."

Brad followed Julie over to the window and leaned slightly toward her to get a better view of Ben's house.

"Sorry, didn't mean to bump you."

"That's okay. I was in your way."

An admonition from years back suddenly began ringing in his ears. To this day he could still hear his father. "Keep your hands in your pockets." He did just that as they left the window to walk out the front door. Brad didn't think he should touch Julie, not just yet.

Once they had dropped Chrissy off, they headed to the Hideaway Cafe built on a bluff overlooking a lake whose blue water matched the sky overhead and reflected the setting sun to the west. A long set of stairs led to its entrance. Julie pushed a buzzer and they were let in. They were shown a table where Brad held Julie's chair for her.

"So, chivalry's not dead yet," she mused to herself. Her thoughts were broken as Brad asked,

"Have you ever lived in a large city or suburb?"

Julie moved the position of her knife and fork on the table in front of her. "I've been to the Cities a few times, but I was born and reared in Milaca."

"You went to school there?"

"Graduated from Milaca High, was active as a pom-pom girl and married shortly after graduation."

"Wouldn't you like the excitement of a big city, cars, busses, people and airplanes overhead?"

"Don't think so."

The conversation changed to the upcoming legal seminar cruise as Brad looked about and leaned slightly towards Julie.

"I rechecked on the cabins available on the cruise ship and found out seminar members have a choice of mini-suites consisting of twin beds with bath along with a sitting room and outside veranda or just a cabin with twin beds and bath."

"Have you made a choice?"

Brad said quietly, "The twin beds with bath, sitting room and outside veranda."

Brad moved closer to Julie, perhaps to avoid being heard by other patrons.

"I understand the ship will move the twin beds against opposite walls and separate the room with a Japanese room divider, but we will have the same bath." Julie's pretension of doubt was helped by resting her chin on her hand.

"Do we know each other well enough to do something like this?"

Julie smiled after the question, and proceeded to answer it herself.

"But it does seem like I've known you for a long time. I enjoy being with you. . . and Chrissy likes you. Besides, I've never been on a cruise of any kind."

The remainder of the dinner was devoted to small talk minus the seminar cruise. They left the cafe and Brad opened the car door for Julie. When they were a few miles from the cafe the silence was broken by Julie turning to Brad.

"Well, I know you're a lawyer, but what are your other interests?"

"I'm in the Air Force Reserves."

"Really?"

"Yes. I serve one weekend a month and 15 active duty days a year."

"How about you?"

"I play softball in a local women's league during the summer, mostly reading in the fall and winter months. So what do you do in the Reserves?"

"I'm a navigator on a C-130 Hercules Airship."

"How long now?"

"Since I got out of law school. Actually, I saw a recruiter in my last year of law school. He suggested I wait until I was finished with school. I went into training at a base in Texas."

Julie looked out the car window. "We're already halfway to my house. Tell me about the training."

"Well, there's physical exercise at the beginning of the day, morning drill with marching or parading to anywhere one would go on the base. In the afternoon we were required to go to four classes for instructions in military history, uniform code, customs and courtesy, and last but not least, health and safety."

"So, what about you, Julie?"

"Oh, I like movies, popcorn, chocolate ice cream and softball."

"Sometime when I'm up this way again we'll go to a movie, eat popcorn, then go to a place that has chocolate ice cream," he said good humoredly. Julie realized they did have some activities in common. She decided to tell him she would go with him.

"Here we are. Turn left at the next corner and we'll be just a hop and skip away from home."

As he drove up to the curb in front of her house, Julie turned and looked at Brad.

"I've been thinking about the cruise. Actually, it's just about all I've been able to think about. I've decided to go with you. Of course, I had some concern what people would say, but now, really, the rumors won't bother me."

Brad smiled, took her hand in his, and said, "Thanks."

She invited him to come in so they could talk further about the cruise. She was surprised at how relaxed and comfortable she felt with him and with the decision she had made. She wondered if he would tell her about what she should wear on such a trip. This was far beyond any of her experiences, and she suddenly realized how uninformed she was about such matters. Brad intuitively sensed that Julie was having such thoughts which prompted him to say,

"I'll find out from the wife of my lawyer friend about clothes and write you after talking to her. They'll be joining us on the cruise."

Winter soon fell over Minnesota and snow covered the land but the highways were clear so Brad drove to Milaca a couple of times during the winter months. He phoned Julie once a week and they talked about their own activities and occasionally about the cruise. Brad promised that he would be sending her a letter after the holidays with information from Mrs. Larimore about the clothes she would be taking on the cruise.

Julie kept a daily watch out her front door window for the mailman, always feeling a bit disappointed whenever a letter didn't arrive. Finally it came.

Dear Julie;

I talked about clothes for the one week cruise with Mrs. Larimore, my friend's wife, who will be joining us on the cruise, perhaps having the cabin next to ours. She will be taking a suit and packing a cocktail dress, two evening gowns, some slacks and blouses for casual clothes, one pair of high-heeled shoes plus a couple of pairs of loafers and sneakers. You will need to be vaccinated for your passport and have flu and malaria shots. Let me know if you need help, financially.

Enjoyed my visits and phone calls. See you soon.

> Your friend with love.
>
> Brad

## Chapter 5

For a number of years after graduation from law school Brad had lived with his parents, brother and sister at their house at the top of a hill in a suburb of Minneapolis. He and his younger brother, Peter, were especially close and frequently played tennis and basketball together on the court on the family property. When Peter left for college, Brad decided to get his own apartment to be closer to his office. John Larimore called it a bachelor's pad after viewing the pictures on the wall, the second bedroom converted into a den with books and magazines filling the homemade bookshelves.

While sitting in a lounge chair, Brad phoned Julie to ask if she got his letter.

"Yes, thanks."

"What do you think of Mrs. Larimore's suggestions?"

"I'll use her ideas and pick up what I need in a larger department store in a nearby town."

"Let me know if you need any money. I'll be driving up again before the month of the cruise. I'll phone you about the date."

Julie beamed with excitement as she talked to Brad on the phone again. When she hung up, she went to her bedroom and viewed herself in the long mirror on the door.

"Can this be happening to me?"

Spring was around the corner and Julie now took more interest in her yard and plans for spring planting of flowerbeds and a garden. She was fond of Brad and felt certain he was fond of her, as well. What she hadn't yet realized was that Brad had fallen in love with her, that he wanted to be with her forever, that life was more enjoyable when he was with her. He wanted to put his arms around her and hold her close to him but his thinking told him, "Keep your hands in your pockets." He didn't feel it was time yet to tell her how he felt about her.

The weekend arrived. Brad visited Julie and discussed the cruise itinerary.

"Julie, let me explain some of the information given to me about the cruise. The cruise begins March 12 and will run for five days. There will be seminars in the mornings with afternoons and evenings free."

Brad could see Julie's face brighten as she clasped her hands on her lap and moved a little forward on the sofa.

"We'll board the Super Liner Cruise Ship after a three-hour flight from Minneapolis." Brad furrowed his brow. "But we have to figure out how to get you to Minneapolis the night before the flight and where you will stay."

"I have a girlfriend living in a suburb of Minneapolis and I'm sure I can stay with her. I'll ask my neighbor to drive me there."

"Good. I'll pick you up at 8 the next morning."

Julie bounced to the phone, called her friend, and asked her if she could stay with her on the night before the flight. It was all set. She gave Brad the address and phone number just as he was saying,

"We're allowed two pieces of luggage each."

"Uh, oh. I didn't even think about luggage. Actually, I don't even have any. Until now, I really haven't had a reason to need luggage."

She stopped a minute, deep in thought.

"The department store where I bought my clothes has some. I'll drive over tomorrow and pick up a couple of pieces."

Julie's independence touched him. He appreciated that she could stand on her own two feet.

"Nobody's ever gonna push her around," he thought to himself.

"Brad, I hate to bring it up, but what about privacy at night?"

Brad swallowed a bit hard, his Adam's apple bobbing up and down in his throat, but he was prepared to answer this question.

"I've arrangements to have a Japanese screen divider set up at night in the center of the cabin between the beds."

A look of skepticism swept over Julie's face as he went on.

"Everything will be okay. I know what you might be thinking, but it won't be that way. I want you to trust me. I'll try to be a gentleman."

Brad looked at his watch.

"It's getting late, almost 9. I think I'll head back to the motel and go over a few files I brought along for an upcoming trial. I plan to visit your neighbor, Ben, in the morning. Would you and Chrissy join me?"

"What time?"

"I'll pick you up at 11 tomorrow morning."

Brad closed his briefcase, walked over to Julie, then kissed her on the forehead and said good-bye to Chrissy.

"See you in the morning."

On Sunday morning, Brad was back at Julie's house knocking on the front door. Julie appeared in her purple sweater and skirt, wearing low-heeled black loafers. Her daughter was dressed in a blue and white pinafore with a white bow in her hair. They slipped on their jackets and the three of them crossed the street to Ben's house where they found him dressed casually, barefooted and reading a book.

Brad introduced himself. "Do you remember me from the trial seminar?"

"Of course. And how are my neighbor girls?"

Chrissy giggled and scampered up to sit next to Ben

on the sofa. He put his arm around her and she cuddled up to him. Ben invited Julie and Brad to sit in the chairs on each side of the fireplace.

"Julie is going to join me in March on a legal seminar conducted on a cruise ship to the Caribbean Islands. There will be seminars on the cruise ship in the mornings and we'll have the afternoons and evenings to ourselves."

Ben smiled.

"That will be a fine trip for both of you, and I know you'll both enjoy the Caribbean Islands. Mrs. Smith and I made a Caribbean cruise a number of years ago and we enjoyed it immensely."

"Julie will be driven to the City where she will stay overnight with a girlfriend and then we'll fly to the east coast to board the cruise ship."

There was no mention of the cabin accommodations or sleeping arrangements, not did Ben ask. They exchanged small talk for a few more minutes.

Brad stifled a yawn.

"It's getting late and I think I should head back to the Cities."

"Thanks for stopping by. Let me know about your trip and take good care of our neighbor girls."

The three walked back to Julie's. Brad walked them both to the door, said good-bye, then walked to his car.

"I'll phone you in a few days and find out how you are progressing in getting your clothes and luggage."

"I'll get everything together, don't worry."

With that Brad got into his car and drove away.

Brad phoned Julie sometime later on. "We'll be leaving in just two weeks. We should get our plans lined up so I can pick you up at your girlfriend's and go to the airport."

Two weeks flew by. Julie and Brad talked on the telephone a couple of times to confirm their plans and the arrangements. Julie had started packing her traveling clothes a week before she was scheduled to leave. She was so excited. She thought about the cruise and the handsome man from Minneapolis she would be with. She was eager to have Brad see her in the cocktail dress and other new clothes. Brad counted the days before he would pick up Julie at her friend's house. He knew he had found the girl of his dreams and that he would always want to be with her. He wondered how Julie felt about him. He got incredibly excited when he thought about being with her every afternoon and at nights.

"I've found her; I'll always want to be with her," he said aloud to himself.

On the morning of the flight, Brad drove to the address given him by Julie. Julie opened the door with her friend standing beside her. Introductions were made. She was wearing a stunning blue striped two-piece suit and blue pumps. Over her suit she wore a tan trench coat. Her lovely dark hair flowed over the high collar of her trench coat as she shook her head to straighten her tresses.

Brad thanked Julie's friend while reaching for her luggage.

"Well, Julie, this is a big day. Soon we'll be flying to the east coast and boarding the cruise ship. Are you as excited as I am? "

Julie appeared exhilarated. "Oh, I can hardly contain myself. This is the first trip I've ever made beyond the Twin Cities."

After arriving at the airport and parking in the ramp, they walked to the counter to check in the luggage. Brad removed the overnight case from Julie's shoulder and carried it for her. Julie had never actually been in an airport before. As Brad handed the tickets to the flight attendant, she heard the attendant ask if they wanted seats together.

They both said "yes" simultaneously and then just grinned at each other.

Brad put his arm around Julie and squeezed her for a second as they walked along. She smiled, reached for his hand and only let go as they walked into the bay. Julie felt a warm flow of happiness when his hand touched hers.

As the plane leveled off, the captain of the airplane reported that they had reached 35,000 feet, the cruising altitude, and that lunch and beverages would be served.

Julie's first airplane ride filled her with some concern but mostly bewilderment.

Brad studied Julie from time to time. She sat next to the window, he in an aisle seat.

"This is incredible, Brad."

"Since the day I met you I always thought about you and me together like this," he said with a warm glow on his face.

Brad leaned over so his shoulder touched hers. Again she smiled as she felt the closeness of his body. She thought of the feeling of security she had when she was with Brad. She recalled that she had never felt this way with another man, not even her ex-husband. She was content.

Their plane landed on the east coast about 4 p.m. After getting a skycap to help with the luggage, they headed for the port of embarkation. They were met at the entrance to the port building by a representative of the Super Cruise Lines wearing a white shipboard uniform. He inquired if they were sailing on the Starfish at 6 p.m. When Brad responded in the affirmative, their bags were picked up by the representative and an aide who took them and lined them up with other bags alphabetically on the floor of the port building.

"We will sail at 6 p.m. sharp, sir. You can board the ship at the stairway. Your suitcases will be placed in your cabin so they will be there when you arrive there."

Julie and Brad walked about on the dock. Julie looked

up at the huge ship in awe. To her it appeared to be a huge white floating hotel standing silently in the dock. It carried twelve lifeboats plus four tenders for 800 passengers and a crew of 750. There were two pools, tennis courts, a casino and a showroom for live shows and a movie theater. A beauty salon and recreation fitness center were among its other amenities. The promenade deck provided ample space for daily walks. The two pools had deck chairs, and cafe tables and bars occupied the spacious stern of the sundeck. As they were walking back and forth on the dock, Brad remembered to ask,

"How did your vaccination and shots turn out?"

"Oh, they didn't bother me at all. I have the reports along with my passport in my handbag," as she opened her bag just to make sure.

Suddenly a blast of the ship horn signaled it was time to board the vessel and Julie and Brad hurried toward the adventure that lay ahead.

*Chapter 6*

As Julie and Brad started for the ramp, they saw John Larimore and his wife. Together they walked up the ramp to the inside of the ship where they were greeted by a hostess who directed them to cabins. They stopped by the information board at ship's entrance to read about services on board. There was a listing of an art and crafts shop, beauty parlor and barber shop, purser's office, skeet shooting, golf practice, swimming pool and movie theaters. Julie was delighted by the ship's amenities. Brad put his arm around her while reading the listing.

"Can we see a movie?" Julie whispered.

"Anything your heart desires," was the response.

Julie and Brad took the elevator to the Sunbeam deck and, finding the direction of their cabin by arrows on the wall, started down the corridor. Brad reached for Julie's hand.

"This apparently is the way to the cabin."

Their cabin was mid-ship on the starboard side. Brad let Julie walk ahead of him. As they reached their cabin door the steward came up and opened it for them.

Julie immediately inventoried the room. There were twin beds against opposite walls, separated by a nightstand with drawers and a large closet and a bathroom with a tub and shower. Off the sitting area there were a sofa and a chair beside a table and lamp. A private veranda on which were two deck chairs with a table in between them faced the ocean.

"Where's the folding screen divider that we were going to put in the center of the room?"

Brad opened the closet door and pointed to the screen standing up against the wall of the closet. The screen was large and sturdy and Julie appeared pleased.

Brad went to one of his pieces of luggage to look for the clothesline while Julie walked over to the sitting room and sat down. As quickly as she had sat down, she immediately proceeded to jump up again and opened the door to the veranda and looked out.

"Brad, this is great! Let's sit out on the veranda later, shall we?"

Brad put his hands on Julie's shoulders.

"Look, Julie. We'll do whatever you'd like. Let's unpack our luggage right now."

As they were hanging up their clothes, Brad remarked. "I forgot to ask you what your choice might be for sitting times for breakfast, lunch and dinner. When the travel agency asked me, I said we would take the second sitting, which would be an 8:30 supper, breakfast at 8 a.m. and lunch at 1 p.m. Is that okay with you?"

"That's just fine with me."

Julie looked around the cabin at the textured carpeting, teak-paneled walls and admired the decor.

"This is a beautiful cabin. Any suggestions as to what I wear tonight?"

"The first night will be casual clothes, perhaps a skirt, blouse. Maybe a sweater for your shoulders if you chill easily."

Julie selected her favorite skirt and blouse with matching shoes, plus a light, white sweater. She started to remove her suit, stopped and said, "Oh! oh! I'd better change in the bathroom."

"No, need. I'll turn my back and look the other way." Julie decided, however, to take her clothes and change in the bathroom. Brad didn't hear any click of the lock on the bathroom door but assumed all was safe so he slipped into some slacks and an open shirt. Brad heard the water running in the bathroom and found himself trying to visualize what might be happening in the shower. He thought to himself, "She's my gal," but to her he offered "You look charming," as she emerged from the bathroom.

Brad decided to grab a quick shower himself. As he came out of the bathroom he mentioned to Julie,

"We'll see the Larimores at dinner. They're seated

with us. You remember seeing John at the Pinewood Cafe?"

"Uh, huh. But I haven't met his wife yet, although you mentioned her name in the letter you wrote me about the clothes."

"They have the cabin next to ours so we'll probably be spending a fair amount of time with them. Is that all right, Julie?"

"Sure. We'll have fun together."

"I'm sure we will. I was wondering if this day would ever come. I enjoy being with you so much, Julie. It's hard to explain. But I will some day." He reached for her hand and escorted her toward the dining room.

The dining room was spacious with seating for groups of eight couples at the long tables, six couples at round tables and two couples at smaller ones. Julie and Brad met the Larimores at the entrance to the dining room where Brad introduced John's wife, Elaine, to Julie. John extended his hand to her. "It's a pleasure to see you again, Julie."

"Thanks. You, too, John. Oh, and Elaine, thanks so much for the tips on what to bring for this trip. I sure appreciate your helpfulness."

Their conversation was interrupted when a waiter walked up and introduced himself.

"My name is Jose' and I will be your waiter at all dining. May I suggest a table for six?" He showed them to their table. A third couple arrived shortly.

John started a conversation about the ship's itinerary.

"Looks like we should arrive at Nassau by early morning." Brad suggested they walk through some of Nassau before breakfast and the start of the seminars. The setting of the sun shown through the portholes in bright colors of red, yellow and blue on the horizon as it cast its rays on the sparkling ocean waters.

"What a sight!" exclaimed Julie as she saw the sun gradually disappearing over the horizon.

Brad followed, "I'm not much of a sailor, but it looks as if it will be a bright and beautiful day tomorrow."

The ship's program for that evening listed a musical presentation by an orchestra in the Pawtucket Room. It was an hour-long program of classical as well as contemporary music. The foursome talked about attending the recital before taking a walk on the Promenade Deck as a prelude to retiring. They asked the third couple to join them but were informed they were meeting friends from their home town.

During the discussion, the husband of the third couple asked,

"Where y'all from?"

John offered the explanation.

"We're from Minnesota. We three from Minneapolis and" pointing to Julie, " Milaca."

"Have any of you ever been to Texas?"

John, "We've been to Dallas-Fort Worth. How 'bout you. Ever been to Minnesota?"

"Not yet, but it's in our travel plans for the future'" the man responded. "Does it really have all those lakes?"

"You bet. There's over 10,000 lakes in Minnesota, flat plains and some rolling hills covered with birch, pine, oak and evergreens. Most of the highways are pretty good, too, if you're driving."

The foursome left for the musical. Brad helped Julie move her chair from the table, put out his arm and Julie slid her arm through his. They walked like that to the musical and on the Promenade Deck with the Larimores before retiring.

As Julie and Brad walked into their cabin, they saw that their beds had been made up for retiring. Julie's lace nightgown and robe with two chocolates in paper cups on them had been laid out on the bed by the steward. Julie was caught off guard.

"I wasn't expecting this!"

"It must be a service of this cruise ship."

Brad felt a pleasurable warmth as he viewed Julie's nightgown on the bed.

"It's a beautiful sleep set you have."

Julie's response was to pick up a chocolate off the lingerie and say,

"Open your mouth. C'mon. Say 'Ahhhh.'"

As she placed the chocolate in his mouth, he closed his eyes hoping she would kiss him. Instead she said,

"A chocolate for you and one for me." She then walked into the bathroom to change.

Brad got out the Japanese screen and set it up between the twin beds. As he checked the screen, he called to Julie, "This should work out fine."

Julie opened the bathroom door slightly, her dark locks, neck and bare left shoulder protruding through the opened door.

"What did you say?"

Brad repeated himself.

"I hope so," as she emerged from the bathroom with her lace robe over her gown.

Brad stood transfixed to the vision before him, a bit dazed as he thought to himself, "My God, she's beautiful." It took him awhile to say, "Excuse me," and head for the bathroom to get in his short pajamas and robe. Julie could hear him singing some oldie whose tune she vaguely recognized.

"Hmmm," she thought, "Cute, and he's got a good voice, too."

He returned to the cabin and sat down in a chair opposite Julie.

"Busy day, huh? Are you tired?"

Julie adjusted her robe. "It's been great fun already. I can't tell you how happy I am that I came with you. It feels like I've known you for quite a while already."

"I have the same feeling, Julie."

"I am getting a little tired now that you mention it."

"We can turn in anytime you want to."

Brad kissed Julie on the cheek. "We'd better get some rest," he said quietly as he headed for his twin bed.

"Good night, Brad. I'll see you in the morning."

The big ship was now out at sea headed for Nassau in the Bahamas where vendors of straw baskets and straw hats were selling their wares along the streets. When Brad looked out the veranda door before retiring, he observed that the sea was getting a little choppy, and white caps were becoming more prevalent as the huge ship plowed through the waves. He did not sense any swaying of the behemoth at that time, but thought to himself that even large ships might indulge in a bit of rolling in high seas. However, with the sound of a light breeze through the airflow vents of the cabin and the sound of waves lapping against the side of the ship, Julie and Brad were both quickly lulled into a deep sleep.

It was close to midnight. All was peaceful. About 2 a.m. Brad was awakened by the rocking of the screen divider caused by the slight roll of the ship. He turned over to get a better view of it when suddenly the divider toppled to the floor with a loud thud. Julie sat bolt upright in bed.

"What in the world happened?"

Brad climbed out of his bed and felt for the light switch in the cabin.

"Don't worry. The divider fell down."

"So it would seem. So now what are we going to do?"

But Brad was distracted more by what he saw in Julie than by the screen falling.

"Julie, you look beautiful tonight. Can I kiss you goodnight again?"

While straightening up in her bed, she placed her hands on her hips.

"What should we do with the screen divider?"

"It's calming down. I'll set it up again."

Brad bent down to kiss her goodnight again but she turned her head so the kiss landed on her cheek instead of her mouth.

As he walked around the screen to his own bed, Julie slid down into her bed again and lay there with a contented smile on her face, satisfied that Brad would give her the time she needed in this relationship. She closed her eyes after throwing back her hair and went back to sleep.

When morning arrived, Brad walked over to open one of the veranda doors to look out on a sky-blue ocean, which now appeared calm and settled.

The ship had anchored in the bay and the passengers were informed they would be taken by tenders to Prince George Wharf in Nassau. Since the ship would not leave Nassau until late in the evening, some of the passengers would spend all day in Nassau. Julie, Brad, and the Larimores planned to make the trip into Nassau on the tender following breakfast and the men's first seminar.

Julie donned a white short-sleeved blouse, blue skirt and white sandals while Brad wore a blue open-neck sport shirt and white slacks along with white loafers.

As Julie stepped from the bathroom she asked, "How do I look? Is this all right for today?"

Brad held up his hand making a sign of "V" for victory, saying, "It won't take me long in the bathroom and then we'll go to breakfast."

Julie turned on the local TV station in Nassau to try to catch some information on tourist attractions. The program highlighted Fort Charlotte, the Queens Staircase, the Royal Victoria Hotel Tropical Gardens, the Rawson Square, and the straw market along with some of the restaurants, among which was the Golden Dragon Patio serving Chinese food. Two things in particular appealed to her, the Tropical Gardens and the Chinese restaurant. She loved flowers; she also loved Chinese food. She couldn't wait for Brad to come out of the bathroom so she could tell him what she saw on TV.

The first session of the legal seminar was brief with time devoted to outlining the sessions, what subjects they would cover and who the speakers would be at each session. The chairman of the seminars was Clyde Anderson, a professor at the law school, who spoke briefly on the new activity on environmental law and family law. Brad and John sat together at the seminars, took notes of the programs for the seminars, and left together after the briefing session.

At the conclusion of the first seminar, the two couples went down to the embarkation deck. A tender was coming across the bay toward the ship. It was larger than a lifeboat, had a roof on it and handled about eighty people. There were a number of other passengers also waiting to be taken into the wharf.

Brad suggested, "Why don't we look at Fort Charlotte before lunch and then tour the other places of interest after lunch?"

The decision was unanimous so they walked to Fort Charlotte and looked at its stone walls and ramparts. The fortified enclosure was built some centuries ago and some of the original cannons were still intact. The ten foot width of the stone walls was the prime subject of conversation among the foursome.

They ate lunch at a Chinese restaurant. After lunch they walked to the Tropical Gardens. The arrangements of exotic orchids, petunias, begonias, dahlias, zinnias, mums, and many other kinds of flowers delighted and excited Julie. She couldn't help but call Brad's attention to them.

"Yes, they are pretty, but they're not nearly as pretty as you."

She looked up at Brad with a smile and he put his arm around her. He wanted to pull her closer to him but hesitated. As they walked around the Tropical Gardens, Julie would grab Brad's hand and pull him toward another flower arrangement, continuously expressing delight.

"What I wouldn't give to make my flower gardens look like this."

"You can. Could I come up some weekend and help you with your garden?"

"I'd love that."

They visited the water tower near Fort Fincastle. Brad commented on the thickness of the stone walls surrounding the three forts on the Island and informed the group that they had to be at least ten to twenty feet in depth. John referred to the brochure he held. "Not only that, but they're built of large granite blocks that weigh over a ton each."

The afternoon drew to a close and Elaine suggested they walk through the straw market at Rawsom Square before going back to the wharf to catch a tender to the ship.

"Pick out a straw hat, Julie. We're going to be in the sun a lot on this trip. Also, you might want to get a straw shopping bag to carry some of our mementos you pick up along the way."

Julie beamed as she walked among the straw hats stacked along side of the walk. She wanted to get one that pleased Brad. Some were priced higher than others. She tried on a few, standing before Brad with each one. She waited for him to say something but he just nodded his head back and forth in disapproval. Then she picked up a small brimmed straw hat with a red band and put it on.

"How 'bout this one?"

Brad stood back a couple of steps. "Uhh, maybe a little wider brim would shade you better."

Julie picked up a couple wider brimmed ones, each banded with a flat top.

"Which one do you like, Brad?"

Brad saw a hat with a red, white and blue band and suggested, "Try on this one."

Julie placed it on her head and turned from one side to the other to give Brad an all around view.

"Perfect. It looks just right on you."

"So, it's this one, is it?"

"Yes, dear, it's you."

Julie smiled and walked closer to Brad. She adjusted the handkerchief in his sport shirt pocket and patted it flat against his chest.

"Thanks, Brad." She was growing extremely fond of Brad.

The ride back to the ship was uneventful until the tender reached the landing platform next to the ship. The tender seemed to bob up and down a bit next to the landing platform As Julie was about to make her step from the tender on to the platform, Brad held her by the elbow to steady her.

As Julie and Brad stepped into their cabin, she noticed the screen divider leaning against the wall. She decided not to say anything about last night's incident. Brad also observed the screen but made no comment. He suggested they invite the Larimores over an hour prior to going to dinner.

"That'd be fun," exclaimed Julie.

"Should I order a bottle of wine?"

Julie's response was slow in coming.

"Actually, Brad, I've never had wine."

Brad was astonished.

"Are you telling me you've never had a beverage with some alcohol in it?"

"Oh, sure. I've had a beer or two with my friends back home."

"But you've never had a glass of wine? Would you prefer a beer?"

Julie seemed puzzled for a moment as to what to say. "No, no, no, Brad. I'll try a glass of wine."

He wondered if Julie was compromising her feelings about drinking wine. He walked over to her. As she stood up, he put his hands on her shoulders. "You sure?" He wanted to put his arms around her, but there was doubt in his mind that she would want him to. Instead, he walked back to his chair and sat down.

"Quite sure." They smiled at one another from across the room.

The second night planned by the cruise line called for semi-formal dress for dinner. Julie glided from the bathroom in a long, white, low-shouldered dress with high-heeled white pumps. Brad awakened from his snooze, shook his head and blinked his eyes.

"Do you ever look beautiful!"

With her shoulder-length brunette locks falling over her exposed shoulders in a low-necked gown, she was a picture of beauty. She smiled.

"You like this then?"

"I'll be very proud to be with you tonight. Julie, my dreams have come true. I've dreamed of somebody like you and here you are standing in front of me."

Julie didn't move. She just stood still except for an occasional brush of her dark locks off her forehead. She was enjoying the praise Brad heaped upon her. Brad continued.

"For years I've wondered if I would find you. That's it Julie. I have found you. There is no one else."

He removed his formal attire from the closet and went into the shower humming the strains of "Always." When he returned he was dressed in a white jacket, black slacks, summer tux shirt with black bow tie, and black shoes.

"So, what d'ya think?"

"Mmmmm, mmmmm. Simply handsome."

"Thanks. Aren't you just being kind."

"No, Brad. I mean it."

"Let's phone John and Elaine and tell them we're ready. Then I'll ring the steward for some wine."

Elaine wore a long, blue gown and John his summer

tux outfit. Both women carried white sweaters to throw over their shoulders. It was an evening of elegance.

The four of them sat around the small cocktail table in the sitting room of the cabin. Brad poured four glasses of fine red wine. John raised his glass.

"Here's to happy seminar days." The clink of their wine glasses reverberated in the room.

"Not bad," commented John. The others nodded, though Julie said nothing.

"What do you think, Julie?" Julie took another sip of wine as Elaine toasted the trip. A few more toasts and the glasses emptied. Julie and Elaine put their sweaters around their shoulders as they left the cabin and headed for the dining room.

Melodies from the Starfish Orchestra were already flowing from the Pawtucket room when the Larimores and Julie and Brad walked in. The foursome looked at one another and smiled knowingly.

"Let's dance."

Julie slipped her hand under Brad's and pulled him aside.

"I'm not very good at dancing. We never did much dancing in Milaca."

"I'll have to hold you a little firmly, but we'll get along all right."

He took her right hand and slid his right hand around her waist. He could feel a little resistance in her body as he tried to hold her. The music was a slow foxtrot beat, so Brad had little difficulty getting Julie to follow his dance steps. That made her smile and relax more in his arms.

Brad looked into her eyes.

"You follow well."

"Thanks." She enjoyed having Brad's arm around her waist as he guided her about the dance floor. Was he her white knight rescuing her from the doldrums of her lifestyle?

Her new-found confidence made Julie feel more comfortable as she passed the Larimores while they were dancing. The music stopped momentarily and the musicians turned their sheet music and commenced playing the Skaters' Waltz. Brad and Julie started up their waltz steps gliding along with the one, two, three rhythm of the music. Julie was more comfortable with the waltz step from weddings she had attended in Milaca.

As they continued their way around the dance floor and were nearing the end of the waltz, Brad put his right arm further around Julie's waist, moving her closer to him. She could feel his closely shaven right cheek against her forehead and hear his breathing in her ear. She felt the fires flicker within and the feeling of warmth and security from his arm around her. She hoped this would go on forever. The music stopped, but her heart kept dancing as she and Brad walked over to the Larimores. It seemed like she might be in a different world, but that one day, unfortunately, the dream could end.

"I feel so much better about my dancing," Julie remarked as they left for their cabin followed by the Larimores.

"How about we take in a few dances when we get home?"

"I'd love that," she said as she reached for his hand.

As Brad opened the cabin door after dinner and walked in, he noticed Julie hesitated for a moment or two. The screen divider stood against the wall. She asked if she could use the bathroom first. Brad noticed the slight change in her attitude and the lack of a smile on her face. While she was in the bathroom Brad positioned the screen divider closer to his bed. Julie returned to the room clad in her nightgown and robe and noticed the divider up.

"Brad," she said quietly, "It's closer to your bed."

"I thought it would be more stable this way. If it does fall, it might not fall toward your bed."

She seemed satisfied with the explanation, removed her robe, got into bed and closed her eyes. Brad slipped into his bed and lay on it with his arms under the back of his head resting on his pillow. He reached to switch out the light in the cabin.

"Julie, can I kiss you good night?"

"That's all, Brad. You know, I'm human too."

"That's all, Julie."

Brad walked around the divider to Julie's bed and knelt down beside her. He put one arm around her waist and the other over her right shoulder and drew her close to him. His lips met hers, a short but meaningful kiss. When he opened his eyes he saw she had her eyes open. He wondered if she had purposely kept them open. As he moved away, he said,

"Julie, I love you."

"I'm happy with you, Brad, but let's go to sleep."

"Alright, Julie. Good night."

Brad walked back to his bed and switched off the cabin light.

Midnight passed and all the cruise passengers, except a few stragglers, were at rest in their cabins. Brad and Julie had turned in before midnight and were sleeping soundly when Brad suddenly got the urge to use the bathroom. In order not to wake Julie, he decided to feel his way to the bathroom. Silently, he put one foot on the floor, then the other, and started to tiptoe toward the bathroom. Suddenly, his right foot and then his upper body touched something.

"It's just the screen," he thought.

With that comment, however, the screen divider fell over to the cabin floor with a noisy landing that awakened Julie. She sat up, a bit startled and confused.

"Brad?"

"I've fallen on the floor."

"What happened?"

Brad had fallen flat on top of the screen and was now rising to his knees and trying to crawl off the screen divider. Brad said in a soft voice, "It's okay. I just knocked over the screen trying to get to the bathroom in the dark. Do you mind turning on the light? I'm sorry. I didn't mean to wake you."

"Are you sure?"

"Julie, you've got to trust me," and with that comment Brad walked into the bathroom and closed the door. Julie then slid down in her bed, turned on her side and closed her eyes. When Brad returned, he tried to set up the screen divider but it had bent and would not stand up again. He laid it down on the cabin floor, climbed into bed quietly, turned off the light, and whispered, "Good night, Julie."

At first, Julie had pretended she had gone to sleep, but then she responded.

"Brad, are you hurt?"

"No, Julie. I'm all right. Thanks for asking."

Brad closed his eyes but thought to himself, "Sure. She cares for me. But how will I know if she loves me when she doesn't tell me?"

Julie and Brad both awakened at 7:30 a.m. which gave them about an hour in which to get ready for breakfast. The ship had arrived at San Juan, Puerto Rico, in the early morning hours. Brad opened the veranda door.

"It's a bright, sunny day."

"Good, I can't wait to see Puerto Rico."

"Listen, Julie. While I'm in the seminar with John,

maybe you and Elaine would like to sit out on the deck or on our veranda."

"I'll ask Elaine what she'd like to do."

"We'd better hurry. We're running a bit late. It's already 8:30."

They walked hurriedly to the Larimore's cabin, knocked on the door and then the foursome went to the dining room for breakfast. There was some hand waving and good morning greetings as they passed along the tables to their assigned seating. The third couple at their table arrived to join them for breakfast.

John, Elaine and Julie were discussing the screen divider when Elaine asked Julie if the divider fell down again.

"Did somebody fall?" It was the wife of the third couple who, until now, had not been terribly interested in the conversation being held at their breakfast table.

Elaine said that nobody was hurt but that she was talking with Julie about a screen divider set up in Brad and Julie's cabin the previous night. This remark immediately prompted the woman to ask why there was a screen divider in their cabin in the first place.

Elaine looked at Julie.

"You want to tell 'em about it, Julie?"

Julie thought about Elaine's question for a second or two. She felt no embarrassment because she and Brad had conducted themselves decently while in the cabin together.

"This is the first outing my friend, Brad, and I have had together since we met some six months ago. We're not married and, well, we felt it was the appropriate thing to do."

The third couple did not belong to the group of lawyers on the seminar cruise so they weren't familiar with the Brad-Julie relationship. After listening to Julie's explanation, the woman offered,

"Well, hon, that's great, but I'm missing the point here. So, why the screen?"

"I guess because the ship did not have any available two bedroom staterooms on it. The ship placed the screen divider in our cabin."

The man suddenly became a bit chivalrous. "There's nothing wrong with that."

Julie smiled. "I guess, truthfully, I was the one who prompted the idea for the screen."

Brad sat back in his chair and listened to Julie describe, with some humor, the screen divider incident. He was proud of the way she handled herself. His wink at her let her know, without doubt, that he approved of what she had said and the way she had said it. He was realizing anew that she could certainly stand on her own two feet and had a mind of her own.

The third couple at the table obviously thought introductions were long overdue in the process of getting acquainted. The inquisitive woman facing Julie spoke up.

"I heard your name is Julie."

Julie nodded and inquired of them, "And your names are?"

The third couple in unison replied, "John and Mabel Sevingist. We're from Austin, Texas."

"John piped up, "That's quite a distance from Minnesota."

"Sure is. So, is it as cold there in winter as we've heard? Lots of snow?"

"Yes, it sure can be. Some years the winters are moderate but we generally get lots of snow and cold weather. We have a lot of outdoor sports to keep us warm, though. We just bundle up for them," chuckled John.

"In Austin we're used to sunshine and warm weather except for a couple of days when it gets down in the lower forties during the winter months."

Brad decided to hop into the conversation. "From May to November the weather in our state gets up into the seventies and eighties; there are over 10,000 lakes, hundreds of resorts, numerous small community celebrations and parades and the Aquatennial celebration in Minneapolis for ten days."

John Sevingist changed the discussion on weather by asking Brad, "Might I ask you what your occupation is?"

"I'm a trial lawyer in Minneapolis, as is John, here. We're with the same law firm. Elaine stays at home and Julie's a waitress."

Brad mentioned that he and Julie had talked about taking in a movie at the ship's theater at 9:30 that evening and later attending the buffet supper held on the promenade deck at midnight. John and Elaine said that they were going to join them after the sing-along with the ship's orchestra.

The movie was entitled Every Time We Say Goodbye with Tom Hanks and Christina Marsillath, a love story relating back to World War II. As the scenes unfolded, Brad moved closer to Julie so that their shoulders were touching. Julie did not move over, but looked at Brad and smiled. He slipped his left hand under her elbow until his hand touched her right hand and then slid his fingers through hers. He squeezed her hand gently, holding it for a long time before releasing it and folding his own hands together. Frequently he would turn his head towards Julie and watch her admiringly. Julie was sensing an intimacy now that she felt she had not previously experienced with him. When the love scenes became more explicit, Julie found herself pressing her shoulder closer to Brad's. Being so close to him gave her a feeling of security and protection.

When the movie ended, Brad noticed that Julie was a little red-eyed although she had admitted that she enjoyed the movie. Brad put his arm through hers and they left the theater. When they entered the cabin, they found the extra white sheets from the steward stacked in the chair which Brad was to use on the clothesline he was to put up in the center of the room.

"Brad, I don't think it's necessary to put up the clothesline."

Brad looked surprised.

"You don't think we need it up tonight?"

"Brad, I trust you. I know you respect me."

He walked toward her, looked her in the eyes.

"Julie, you know I never do anything to harm you or take advantage of you. It's sometimes hard to explain my feelings toward you. I just want to be with you all the time. It feels like you're the only one for me."

Both prepared for bed. Julie climbed into bed, but remained sitting up.

Brad walked over to her bed and knelt down as he had the night before. He did not ask her if he could kiss her. Instead he put his arms around her and she reached up putting her arms around him. Pressing their lips together, they hung on to each other until Julie released her arms and they separated.

Julie, somewhat out of breath, said "Brad, you mean a lot to me."

"Julie, I love you."

"I'll see you in the morning," as she pulled her comforter to her chin.

They both awakened to voices on Pier 3 where the Prince Starfish had docked in San Juan, Puerto Rico. Brad walked over to the veranda door, opened it and looked out at the crowd of people milling around the dock.

"Looks like another great day."

After breakfast Brad and John attended the morning seminar, while Julie and Elaine went through the gift shops on the ship. Then they attended a lecture in the theater of the ship on "St. Thomas Island, American's Caribbean Playground."

Brad had suggested that the women might want to shop in downtown San Juan after the lecture on St. Thomas Island. They all agreed to meet for lunch at the Intercontinental Hotel at noon. Julie and Elaine discussed the bright colored patterns of greens, reds and gold found in the dresses in women's stores. They walked into a couple of men's stores to check out the white linen slacks, striped lined suits and sport shirts of various patterns. They looked but made no purchases since they were shopping mainly for ideas.

Following lunch the foursome set out for the El Morro Castle on a bus tour prearranged by the cruise ship. The El Morro Castle had been built in stone with walls 20 feet thick surrounding a parade grounds and living quarters for hundreds of soldiers. The fort had not changed since the 15th century, when it was used to protect against pirates and enemy invaders.

They visited the rain forests in the hills outside San Juan. Julie showed her love of flowers as she knelt down to look at the exotic nature all around her. The rain fell lightly and continuously on the plants and flowers, only enhancing their beauty.

The foursome returned to the ship about mid afternoon. Julie and Brad returned to their cabin. He suggested they relax out on the veranda and just enjoy the ocean view. Julie removed her shoes and socks and Brad followed suit. A slight breeze fanned them and they decided to sit out on the veranda until almost dinner time.

"What do you think our live will be like after this week is over?"

"I don't know, Brad. You'll go back to Minneapolis to your law firm, and I'll go back to Milaca and the Pinewood Cafe."

"But I've got to see you, Julie."

"I want to see you too, Brad."

"Can I drive up on the weekends I don't have to go to the reserves?"

"I love that, except that I work some weekends."

"I'll phone you, and you can let me know which weekends you work. Because of the trial work my week days are relatively unpredictable."

After dinner Brad, Julie and the Larimores went down to the Pawtucket room, watched some of the passengers compete in a contest for the best dressed calypso dancer and then proceeded to dance to the Starfish orchestra. Brad held Julie a little closer than the previous dance evening, placing his cheek against hers as they glided around the dance floor to the soft music. Julie was again feeling a sense of comfort and security in Brad's arms. Thoughts whirled through her head of being with him forever. She seemed to conclude her thoughts by saying to herself "It's all a dream," but she knew she was there on the dance floor in his arms. She sometimes wondered what the future, if any, would be between them.

After a late night snack they retired, again with no screen or sheets. Brad knelt over Julie's bed and kissed her on the lips.

"Good night. I'll see you in the morning."

The following morning the ship arrived and docked at the West Indian Company Wharf within walking distance of the shopping area of St. Thomas Island. Instead of having breakfast on the ship, the foursome walked the distance to the city of Charlotte Amalie so they could eat at Sebastian's Restaurant. It was a unanimous decision to take a brisk walk barefooted along the shore, between the wharf and the city. Brad helped Julie over some of the stones along the shore and frequently slipped his arm under hers as they walked. Sebastian's specialized in fruit breakfasts. A plateful of orange slices, pieces of pears, grapes and whole bananas were placed before them along with blueberry muffins and coffee. It was a veritable tropic feast which more than satisfied their hunger after their pre-breakfast exercise.

The main street of Charlotte Amalie was the center of most of the shopping activity on the island. Certain shops on the main street caught one's attention with their colorful signs hanging out over the sidewalks. Prominent merchants on St. Thomas Island were A.H. Riise liquor store, with its many varieties of liquors, Nassau Shop, of men and women clothing, and Mahogany Crafts with its wood carved statuettes. Following breakfast, Brad and John returned to the ship for the seminar and made plans to meet the ladies at 12:30 at the Ocean Cafe for lunch.

Julie and Elaine decided while in San Juan that they would make their purchases in St. Thomas. They went directly from breakfast to a women's store where they milled around looking at the racks of apparel. At Mahogany Crafts Julie saw some hand-carved mahogany miniature statues of natives.

"I'd like a couple of these for my knick-knack shelves," Julie gleefully announced with an almost childlike excitement.

At noon the foursome met and had sandwiches and a fruit drink.

"You'd look great in a sport shirt I saw here while Elaine and I were browsing," she said to Brad with a bit of a twinkle in her smile. "I saw some small mahogany statues in one of the shops I'd like to pick up, too."

Brad reached across the table and put his hand on Julie's.

"Anything your little heart desires. But should we look at some of the sights first and then shop?"

"Sure, Brad, if that's okay with Elaine and John."

Elaine and John nodded in unison. "Sounds good to us. Let's sightsee a while."

They headed for Bluebeard's Castle and the beach club on a hilltop that overlooked the town from which they could see the blue waters of the bay and the boats that filled the harbor. The front of the castle was a 300-year-old stone tower that served as an entrance backdrop to the resort. They walked through the Pirate's Parlor Cocktail Lounge and along the seaside terraces of the resort. The seaside terraces of Bluebeard's club from the heights of the bay caught Julie's eye. If she saw something exciting to her, she took Brad's hand and led him directly to it.

They walked about St. Thomas Island to view the other different resorts built along the coast line of the island. The chair of Sir Francis Drake built high on a hill permitted them a full view of St. John's Island nearby.

Julie led the group towards the Mahogany Crafts again because she wanted to look at some of the miniature carved mahogany statues. She found one about four inches high of a native woman carrying a basket on her head. While she was looking at this particular carving, Brad summoned a clerk in the store.

"I think the lady would like this statue."

Julie nodded her head and the clerk wrapped it for her. Brad paid for it and they left to browse other shops.

"Thanks, Brad."

When the four entered Cavanagh's, both Julie and Elaine started looking at dresses and Brad and John followed them around the store. The women spent some time around the brightly flowered dresses. Both Brad and John asked the women if they wanted any particular dress.

"Oh, Brad, you shouldn't be doing this too," as she smiled and fingered the flowered dress of her choice. "I'll reimburse you when we get back to the cabin," and proceeded to pick out a sun dress for Chrissy.

A clerk folded the dresses in separate boxes. The clerk was paid and they walked to other shops in the downtown area. Time flew by and suddenly Brad looked at his watch only to realize that they should be getting back to the ship.

## Chapter 7

THEY ARRIVED BY CAB at the wharf. They gazed at the huge ship, awestruck by its length and height. People were sitting on their verandas, some even waved at them.

"Tomorrow morning the ship leaves for Florida, the end of our trip, and we'll be at sea almost two days. Tonight is casual dress, but tomorrow night will be the gala farewell ball, which will be formal."

By now they had reached their cabin. Julie seemed to be day dreaming and stared almost absentmindedly at the cabin wall.

"Penny for your thoughts, Julie."

"Oh, Brad, I just can't believe this is going to end. It feels too soon."

"There will be places to go again." Brad replied tenderly.

Julie nodded off in one of the cabin chairs. About a half-hour later she awoke with a start to find Brad kneeling beside her looking at her. She sat up straight.

"What's up?"

Brad had sat out on the veranda reading the ship's paper while Julie rested but it was time to awaken her for dinner.

"You dozed off. I didn't want to startle you by calling out your name to wake you."

He took her by the hand and helped her out of the chair. As she stood, he put his hands gently on her shoulders.

"One of these days I want to have a talk with you about you and me; about our future."

He leaned down to kiss her and she moved in closer to let him. As they embraced, Brad entwined his hand in her hair and pulled her tightly against himself. Julie felt herself melting in his arms, a feeling she hadn't had in many, many years. It felt wonderful; it felt frightening. She pulled away.

"I'd better hurry and get ready for dinner."

Once in the bathroom, she looked at herself in the mirror and mumbled aloud "My, God. Am I falling in love?"

"What did you say?"

"Oh, nothing. I'll be out in a minute."

Following dinner Brad, Julie and the Larimores decided they had had enough excitement for the day and decided to spend a relaxing evening in the ship's theater watching a movie.

After the movie the foursome decided a walk on the Promenade Deck would be the perfect end to a perfect day. As they reached the stern of the great ship, they stood at the railing watching the lights of the city of Charlotte Amalie across the harbor. Julie didn't say much, but stood near Brad looking at the city with longing eyes and a forlorn expression.

"Is something wrong, Julie?"

"No, not really. I'm just trying to build a picture in my mind of what we're leaving behind."

Brad put his arm around her.

"There will be another day."

The moon shone brightly over the deep blue waters of the Caribbean as if competing with the glow from the city. The lights of smaller craft glittered like sparklers as they slowly moved about the harbor. It was a warm, comfortable evening which only enhanced the picturesque scene from the stern of the ship.

Julie and Elaine excused themselves for a few moments, leaving Brad and John in conversation.

"John, I'd like to get your take on Julie and me. I think we're building respect and love for one another in a healthy and wholesome kind of way. I've never quite felt like this before, but my love for her seems to have quelled any sexual prowess I normally would have had in this kind of situation. I've purposely even stayed away from alcohol so I'd be in control of myself."

As the women walked toward them, John whispered, "I think you're doing it right, Brad."

There was little conversation between Julie and Brad

as they all walked together back to their cabins except for comments about the beautiful evening, everyone's tiredness and desire to turn in. A kiss goodnight and Brad's remark about loving Julie before they got into their beds completed the evening.

With the dawn of a new day, the sun shone brightly through the veranda doors and lit up the entire cabin. Brad awakened first and let Julie sleep while he slipped quietly into the bathroom. Julie awakened to the sound of the shower and looked about the cabin. Then she slid down under the covers and tried to go back to sleep.

"Julie, wake up, you sleepyhead."

She pretended not to hear him for awhile, then sat up in bed.

"Good morning, Brad. The ship is moving. Are we on our way back?"

"We'll be at sea today, tonight and part of tomorrow. We should arrive in Florida tomorrow evening."

"I think while you're at the seminar, I'm going to call for an appointment at the beauty shop to have my hair done for the ball tonight." Brad left for the seminar and Julie spent the rest of the day in the relaxation of uneventful activities aboard ship.

At the farewell banquet they toasted each other with Mai Tais at dinner before the final dance. The passengers seemed quieter and more subdued than the previous nights. Everyone's expressions were a bit sober; the end was nearing and they were all feeling its effects.

Brad and Julie held each other closely and tightly in their final dances. She put her head on his shoulder as they danced the last waltz to Auld Lang Syne.

"I love you, Julie. . . always will."

She beamed as she put her arm through his and walked from the ballroom to their cabin. They quickly dressed in their night clothes. When Julie returned to the cabin from the bathroom, she saw a package lying on her bed.

"Surprise!" Brad exclaimed from his chair.

She opened the package to find a floor-length, over the shoulder dress of bright floral colors of red, green and yellow. She walked over to Brad and knelt down before him.

"Brad, how can I thank you, not only for the dress but for an incredible time together these past days."

He leaned over and lifted her up from her kneeling position as he raised himself from the chair. He had his arms around her and kissed her, at first gently, but progressively with more passion. He could feel the closeness of her body pressed against his, separated only by a lace negligee and robe. He wanted to love her. They kissed for a long time. He longed for her but he knew how she felt. He quietly suggested they retire. They did, each to his own bed.

Brad twisted and turned about on his bed for a long time. He could not get to sleep. He slipped out of his bed and walked silently over to the side of Julie's bed.

She also was still awake, unable to sleep. He knelt down besides her.

"Julie, are you asleep?"

He slipped off his undershirt.

"Brad, what are you doing?" Julie whispered with a voice that virtually pleaded for an explanation.

He slid his body into her bed as she turned herself around so that she was facing the cabin wall. Brad slipped his right arm around her and turned her towards him so that they were facing each other. He pulled her toward him and kissed her cheeks and mouth.

"Please, Brad, I can't," but her protestations were weak and seemingly insincere.

He kissed her again and again while telling her "I love you."

She slipped her arms around him. Gently and tenderly he lifted her gown over her head and removed his shorts. He leaned into her neck and moved slowly downward toward her breasts. She offered no resistance. He lovingly turned her on her back.

The waves lapping against the hull of the ship produced a rhythm that reached the cabin and enveloped Julie and Brad. A quietness fell over the cabin with only the rhythm sounding like the rise and fall of a wind. Eventually a contented silence fell over the cabin. They slept in each other's arms.

The light of a new day filtered into the cabin awakening Brad. He remained still as he listened to the breathing of Julie in a deep sleep. He did not want to awaken her. Slowly and gingerly he lifted himself out of bed and walked silently to the bathroom. He hoped the noise of the shower would not awaken Julie so he turned the shower to a trickle and decided not to shave until later. When finished in the bathroom he opened the door slightly to see if Julie was still sleeping. He picked up a magazine and sat out on the veranda. Nearly two hours later he heard the bathroom door close and the shower turn on. Julie stepped out on the veranda in her terry cloth robe fluffing her hair with a towel. Brad watched her as she walked toward him.

"Good morning, Julie."

Julie smiled as she said, "Did you sleep well?"

Brad put aside his magazine. "Great. How about you?"

"Wonderfully. Was I dreaming or did you tell me you loved me?"

"I did. . . and I do, Julie, with all my heart and soul."

They returned to the cabin to pack, but the aura which surrounded them for the rest of the day was unmistakable, undeniable. Their hearts had connected, and they would never be the same for it.

Julie's girlfriend was at the airport to meet her. Brad took Julie by the hand and led her aside where they could talk privately before they had to part.

"Julie, you'll never know how much it meant to me

to have you joining me on the cruise. I hope you had as wonderful a time as I did. I want to see you again, soon, but I have to get back to trial work and plans for the summer State Bar Association convention, so it probably won't be as soon as I'd like."

"I'll miss you, Brad. Please, call me soon."

As she departed, she turned back to see Brad watching her leave. She waved good-bye, again, and hoped that he saw in her smile her desire to be with him again soon.

*Chapter 8*

TWO MONTHS AFTER Julie and Brad returned from the cruise, Ben called to ask if she would be interested in driving with him to the Minnesota State Bar convention in Duluth. They would leave in the morning and return the same day before dinner. Julie agreed and said she'd be looking forward to attending a style show that would be offered.

"Should I wear the same clothes I wore on the cruise with Brad?"

"That'd be fine."

Brad had been selected as a speaker at the convention on the phase of the program devoted to trial before a court and jury.

Life returned to normal for Julie once the cruise was over. She went back to work at the cafe and to the lifestyle she had before the spring cruise, spending most of her non-working time with Chrissy. Brad phoned her each weekend and in one of the last conversations they had had, he explained that he had not invited her to the convention because she would be alone most of the time. His duties in organizing and then daily supervising the scheduling and timing of events left him little, if any time, for social activities. Though retired, Ben generally attended the convention in the summer if it was held in Duluth. He was looking forward to the trip.

Brad's presentation was scheduled for the first meeting following a luncheon in the ballroom of the Downtown Hotel which was within walking distance of the convention center. At the luncheon, Brad sat at the head table with the MC of the convention and other speakers along with the State Bar Association officers. Ben and Julie joined a group of lawyers and their wives at a table located almost in front of the speaker's podium of the head table. Brad was seated left of the podium in a location that made it necessary to look around the podium to view the woman and the man who were sitting with their backs to the head table.

The master of ceremonies introduced the persons sitting at the head table. Each stood to be viewed by the audience. As Brad was introduced, he stood and looked at the woman and man who had turned half way around in their chairs to watch the introduction. Brad gazed at the couple.

Throughout the course of the luncheon, Brad would stretch across the head table to look around the podium to catch Julie's attention. She, in turn, would turn her head around toward him and occasionally their eyes would meet before she would suddenly turn back and commence a discussion with the old man beside her.

After the luncheon, a style show was staged for the female lawyers, and lawyers' wives. Brad went to the table where Julie and Ben were sitting and spent a few minutes in discussion with them. After Brad left for the convention center, Ben escorted Julie to the style show and then left for the convention center.

The afternoon seminar was scheduled for 2 p.m. Brad was introduced as the speaker, with the Master of Ceremonies explaining the nature of Brad's presentation. Brad said he would first tell about his experience in trial work and the impaneling of a jury.

Twenty minutes into the style show, Julie sneaked out and went up to the registration counter of the hotel where she asked how to get to the convention center. Once inside the center Julie inquired where the seminar on trial advocacy was being held. She was directed down the hall. As she pulled back one of the large doors to the room to peek inside, she could hear Brad speaking. She slipped into the room and was about to sit down at the rear of the room when Brad suddenly stopped speaking. She caught his eye just as he was looking at her. He said nothing for a couple of seconds, then concluded his presentation. Julie was thrilled to hear the applause he received.

He left the podium and proceeded to Julie's table.

"Julie, I didn't know you'd be here. I just assumed you'd stay at the style show."

"I wanted to come over and listen to your presentation."

Brad placed his hand upon Julie's.

"Why don't we take a walk up to the park along the channel that leads into the Duluth harbor."

As they walked down the main avenue of Duluth, they momentarily stopped and looked in the windows of various shops along the street. They both stopped at the window of a jewelry store and discussed the beauty of certain pieces being displayed. Julie looked away from the window and turned her head towards the sky of deep blue. The sun shone brightly with its rays slightly slanted on a diamond in the window. The diamond danced with a brilliant, luminous and sparkling color. Suddenly, and inexplicably, she felt a desire to possess it. The feeling frightened her and she stopped herself when she realized that it was only something she could look at and never have.

Once they reached the bridge street, they turned right and walked the few blocks toward the lift bridge park. At the far end of park was a small bench. They sat down, neither saying anything for a moment or two until Brad turned toward Julie and broke the silence.

"You can't know how glad I am to see you again, even if it is at another convention. I'll bet Ben figured we'd see each other. Sly old fox!"

Julie giggled aloud.

"Ben needed me to help him drive back and forth to the convention, which is some distance from Milaca. I'm so glad I came. I couldn't wait to see you again. He's only planning to attend the convention today, but, who knows, he could change his mind and attend tomorrow, too."

Brad put his arm on the back of the bench behind Julie's shoulders. Then he slipped his arm down around her and drew her closer to him. He leaned into her so that his head touched hers. He had not had his arm around Julie since the cruise. She snuggled into him. It gave her a feeling of security and warmth.

"Do you know how often I think of you? No other woman has ever given me the enjoyment and pleasure you do. I've never felt this way about any other woman. You're on my mind constantly. You've captured my heart. I miss you when we're not together."

"Even knowing that I have been married and divorced and that I have a young child by that marriage?"

Brad smiled tenderly. "Yes. After I saw you at the cafe in Milaca, I heard about your divorce. It doesn't change my feelings for you."

Julie's expression changed. "I've thought of you more than you'll ever know."

He took her hands in his and gently kissed her on the cheek. She tucked her head against his neck and nestled it on his shoulder. They both sat as if in a spell.

Suddenly they heard the blast of a ship's horn. Off in the distance on the huge lake was a large ore vessel headed for the channel. They watched as it neared the entrance to the channel. It moved slowly and passed the bench where they were sitting. It was a monstrous vessel, two blocks in length, sitting high in the water. There were numerous hatches on its deck with large living quarters and operational quarters forward and aft. The water line was about six feet above the water as it entered the channel, indicating it was coming in to take on cargo, perhaps coal or taconite at the docks in the inland harbor at the other end of the channel.

Once the ship passed through the channel, Julie and Brad headed back to the main street of the convention city. While walking towards the convention center, Brad casually suggested, "Let's stop in front of that jewelry store just once more."

There was a little glimmer in his smile.

Meanwhile, Ben had chanced across some of his longtime friends who had practiced law in Minneapolis at the same time he had. One of them told Ben he'd like to go for a walk and look for a comfortable corner in the closest hotel where they could sit and talk about the past together.

While visiting with his friends, Ben realized he had not seen Julie since he left her at the style show. He mentioned that he had better start looking for her so they could start for home. Not finding her at the style show, he went, on a hunch, to the convention center.

Sure enough, Julie and Brad were walking down the hall looking at memorabilia displays. Ben asked Julie how she had enjoyed the style show.

"Oh, I left after fifteen or twenty minutes and went to the seminar to hear Brad speak. Once he finished, we walked to the channel park. Brad has suggested that we come back again tomorrow. There will be a good luncheon and a boat tour around the islands. I'm sure I can get the same sitter for my daughter."

Ben turned to Brad with a bit of a knowing smile. "We'll meet you in the hotel lobby at noon."

Ben and Julie walked to the car in the parking lot to head home for Milaca. The drive took about two hours. Ben let Julie off at her home and drove across the street to his own place. Chrissy and the sitter met Julie at the door. It had been a good day. Who knows what tomorrow would hold?

*Chapter 9*

THE NEXT MORNING brought a bright and sunny day with temperatures predicted to be in the seventies. Ben picked up Julie about mid morning for the drive back to Duluth. They planned to meet Brad for lunch.

Brad was standing outside the hotel as they arrive. The three went to lunch together where they were treated to a menu of chicken breasts, green beans, small white potatoes and a dessert of ice cream and strawberries. Following the luncheon a short meeting took place in which the guest speaker, a female Judge of District Court, spoke on suggestions for reducing the backlog of civil cases on the court calendars.

Immediately following the luncheon and the address, the master of ceremonies announced that an excursion boat would take some of the guests around the sound on a tour of the various docks and out into the lake among the Disciple Islands. The boat would sail in an hour.

Brad suggested that he and Julie wait for the sailing

by sitting on a bench facing the harbor just outside the convention center.

"Julie, I want to see you more often. Since the cruise I've been constantly in trial during the week and on extra duty on weekends at the Air Force Reserves. It's been terribly difficult to get away."

"I'd like that, too, Brad. Let's try to work it out." There was a tug on her heart to tell Brad more as to how she felt about him but the words would not come.

The sightseeing boat docked near the convention hall. It had two enclosed decks with wide view glass windows, and accommodated up to 300 persons. It was used primarily for an excursion of the lake among the Disciple Islands and the inland port of the harbor, providing sightseeing for the passengers. It also offered buffet luncheons and moonlight cruises. There were two stairways from the enclosed decks forward and aft, plus an open deck that permitted passengers to view the sights in the port and lake from outside the first and second decks. The pilot house was at the front of the third deck.

Life preservers for all passengers and crew members were inserted in between the rafters or ceiling beams of the cruise boat and could be released from their supports by a tug on the jacket. On the stern of the boat there was a waist high metal railing that permitted passengers to walk about and view the sights. The excursion boats were built of riveted steel plates and two decks enclosed with unbreakable glass windows. The boats were powered by two large diesel engines operated from the pilot house. There were a number of A Type IUV PFDs designed to be thrown to a person in the water should someone fall overboard. The excursion boat was licensed, inspected and approved by the United States Coast Guard.

The cruise boat was to leave at 2 p.m. sharp and would return at 4 p.m. Ben suggested that Julie and Brad go together as he had planned to join some of his old acquaintances. Brad and Julie walked down to the dock from the bus holding hands the whole while. Brad assisted Julie onto the boat and they both were greeted by the familiar voices of their friends, the Larimores, who had stepped onto the boat just a few moments before them.

The foursome walked to the bow while engaged in conversation. Julie's hair sparkled in the sun's rays. She looked radiant in her blue-green skirt and blouse, which brought out a special glow in her dark hair. Brad looked especially sporty in his double-breasted blue-striped jacket, open neck off-yellow sports shirt and off-white trousers. Julie's locks swirled around and across her face from the breeze. Brad occasionally would reach over and gently brush her hair off her face.

As the breeze continued to whip Julie's hair, it also left her feeling chilled. Brad helped her put her sweater on as they walked toward the bow of the boat. They could hear the refrains from the entertainment aboard. Julie suggested they walk inside the enclosed lower deck. The breeze was getting even stronger as the boat moved further out into the harbor. As she and Brad walked along the deck, she also noticed a few waves on the water and an occasional whitecap.

She put her arm in Brad's, hanging on to him tightly. The boat glided close into shore, past large grain elevators, huge coal and ore docks and past numerous cargo ships docked ready to be loaded. The tour boat was not as big as a ferry, but was larger than any yacht sailing the inland waters. Dock workers were guiding chutes used for moving grain and ore into the holds of the ships. The ship's water lines rose as the holds were filled.

For the skipper of the excursion it would be another uneventful day as he piloted the boat into the harbor near the large elevators and docks. He absentmindedly listened to the rhythm of the two large diesel engines as they turned the screws propelling the boat through the water.

The harbor and some of the waters near the Disciple Islands outside the harbor had been dredged many years ago. Periodically topographical engineers surveyed the areas to determine if additional dredging was necessary. In such tranquil and smooth waters it hardly seemed likely that anything could happen to the boat, or to its happy and talkative passengers. There had never been a calamity in the operation of the excursion boats in the lake among the Disciple Islands or in the bays where they operated, and any disruption of their safe return to the boat docks near the convention center was certainly not anticipated by any of the crew.

As the excursion boat moved along, the breeze picked up. Julie and Brad chatted about the few whitecaps that appeared near the channel in the inland harbor. Julie noticed that other women were trying to escape the chill by donning sweaters or moving inside enclosures. Within one-half hour into the tour, the wind intensified. As the sky became more overcast, small gatherings of passengers began to converse about the change in the weather, and there was an occasional remark about the growing size of the waves lapping against the hull of the boat. Brad noticed the water was becoming choppy and the air cooler.

Julie and Brad walked outside and stood on the bow of the ship with John and Elaine. They decided to walk to the aft deck where they stood along the rail surrounding the boat's stern. Suddenly the winds shifted and it became more apparent to all that the weather was changing for the worse and that the water was becoming more and more choppy by the minute.

Off in the distance coming from the direction of a large ore dock was a large ore boat with a red painted bow and white lower deck, its upper deck and pilot house atop the bow looming above the water as it moved into the bay. Julie motioned to Brad.

"Wow, it sure is riding low after taking on a load at one of the docks."

The excursion boat's bow was now headed through the ship channel opposite the elevators and docks and into the great lake among the Disciple Islands. As they viewed the other vessels that were still in the harbor, Brad commented again to Julie and the Larimores that it appeared the large coal or ore vessel was also headed toward the channel. It was moving at about five knots but was becoming more obvious because of its size and the slight roll of the waves, which were increasing in height as they lapped against the hull of the great ship.

Their attention was shifted from the waters to the voice now coming over the loudspeaker. The guide informed them that outside the harbor beyond the channel is the largest inland fresh water lake in the country. Ten islands called the Disciple Islands arise from the waters within 15 miles of the entrance to the channel and harbor. These islands are some miles apart with water depths between them that permit large ocean-going vessels to travel among them. However, reefs and rocky shorelines extend out from some of the islands, which gave rise to the explanation of the buoys which were in evidence in the waters between the islands.

The islands varied in size, some being six miles long and three miles wide while the smallest was one mile long and about one-half mile in width. Some of the islands were covered with evergreen forests and others had outcroppings of large areas of granite. Some old logging camps and stone quarries were visible to passengers. The outer islands had lighthouses and quarters for permanent lighthouse personnel on the far end of the islands facing the open expanse of the great lake.

It was a common sight to see large commercial vessels and other craft, including excursion boats, plying the waters between the islands. The excursion boats usually were navigated across such waters from island to island so their passengers could get a better view of each island. For a pilot of a large ore carrier to negotiate the waters between the islands crowded with cruise boats and other pleasure craft was a severe test of that pilot's ability. The excursion boat pilot had to steer the ship close enough to the islands to give the passengers a chance to take photographs. To do this the excursion boat sometimes came close to the reefs or rocky ledges of the islands.

"It probably will be rougher out in the open lake than in the harbor," Brad offered pensively.

Julie buttoned her sweater around her, anticipating the chill of sea air against her.

As both boats cleared the channel and headed for the open lake and Disciple Islands, they encountered rougher water and large, cresting waves. The wind had increased dramatically and the sky grew darker and more ominous.

As the excursion boat proceeded on its way amongst the islands, Brad nudged John.

"Look. The large ore boat we saw leaving the dock along the harbor is close to clearing the ship channel to head out to open lake."

Brad had barely finished his sentence when he heard the long and short horn blasts from the pilothouse of the ore boat. They all watched as the lift bridge was raised to accommodate the huge ore boat to pass under it and through the channel.

By now, their own boat was passing among the Disciple Islands with the captain explaining some history about each island. Those islands on which logging had been an industry around the turn of the century and those on which quarries had operated were pointed out to the passengers as the boat meandered close to give the passengers a better view. The side walls of the quarries were smooth and shiny, indicating great slabs of stone had been chiseled from them. Large chunks of stone removed from the quarries were standing in piles along part of the shoreline. No explanation was given as to why they had remained there and had not been taken from the island.

On the islands on which logging had been conducted years back, one could still see the mess hall quarters and sleeping quarters of loggers standing in silent memory of the old logging days. The logging was carried on during the winter months when the great lake was frozen solid enough to transport the men and logging sleds pulled by horses across it to the mainland. Breakwaters and docks extended out into the lake from numerous islands providing protection and loading facilities for any industry on the islands.

As the boat was leaving the last island to head back towards its base, it passed close to the shoreline to give the passengers a good view of the lighthouse and living quarters of the lighthouse keeper.

Brad looked down into the water. "I hope we don't get too close to shore. I can see the rocks."

The sightseeing boat had dropped its speed for passengers to get better photos. While cruising at a slower speed, Brad suddenly bumped John with his arm.

"Hey, did you feel that?" A grinding noise at the rear of the boat made him think aloud, "I think we've hit some rocks."

Just then the excursion boat lost its momentum and seemed to drift.

The captain of the tour boat used the radio to call for help. He announced his location as middle of Disciples Islands.

Both Julie and Elaine voiced their concern as they listened to the conversation between Brad and John. The two women sought some comfort in huddling together under the ship's blanket the men had retrieved from a small closet inside the tour boat.

Brad looked around and saw passengers on the second

deck coming down the aft stairway in a hurry with concerned expressions on their faces. As they milled about at the foot of the stairs, the question among many was "What caused the boat to quiver for a second?"

As if the captain had heard their question, suddenly the loudspeaker broke the hum of peoples' concerns. He explained that it felt like the screws and rudder had hit some rocks and may have been twisted or damaged.

"There's nothing to worry about, folks. The rudder seems intact and we can guide the boat into the closest dock. There are life belts stored in the rafters and along sides of the walls. Just to be on the safe side of things, I suggest each of you put one on."

Crew members immediately began to hand out life belts with instructions to each passenger as to how to use them. For a few brief moments the boat lay idle in the water, but the waves were beginning to make it sway, much to the consternation of most of the passengers.

Brad helped Julie put on a life belt over her sweater. The Larimores also put on their life belts. Brad tried to make small talk to divert Julie so he pointed to a large vessel headed out from the channel in the direction of the excursion boat.

The officers on the bridge of the ore vessel could see that the excursion boat appeared to be adrift and in trouble. The pilot gave two long blasts on the ship's horn and appeared to slow down. The breeze, which was gentle at the beginning of the cruise, had now increased to such intensity that it was causing the boat to sway and move listlessly in the water as it was pushed by the waves.

John was the first to comment on the new turn of events. "Oh, oh. The waves are pushing us sideways. Looks like we're drifting toward the channel."

His assessment was quite accurate. At that same moment, the officers of the large ore vessel realized that the excursion boat was floating aimlessly and uncontrollably toward it.

From the pilot house of the excursion boat came the sharp emergency blasts of its whistle.

A fierce wind was churning the waves into whitecaps. The excursion boat was now helplessly moving in the waves which were rocking it back and forth. As Brad and Julie watched from their positions at the rail of the stern, they observed a number of passengers coming down the steps with bewildered and fearful looks on their faces. Others seemed excited and confused. More and more passengers pressed down the steps onto the stern until the overflow were left standing on the steps. Looking into the sky, Brad observed that clouds were getting darker and lower.

"There's a squall or storm developing and it looks like we're right in the midst of it."

"Hate to admit it, but I think you're right, buddy," said John shaking his head unbelievingly.

The rolling of the excursion boat in the waves was

beginning to create havoc. Plastic and paper cups, along with boxed popcorn, were coming off the counter and rolling on the deck of the boat. Men and women hung onto one another to steady themselves against the rocking of the boat.

Brad put his arm around Julie to steady her as they leaned against the stern's railing. He took her free hand in his and felt a slight tremble as he held it.

"Do you think we'll be blown in the course of the ore boat?" queried John who noticed that the ore boat now seemed to be fewer than 300 yards away.

Fear of impending danger shown on the faces of the passengers also standing on the stern of the boat as it bobbed and turned sideways in the rough water. Five short blasts came from the ore boat, apparently aware of the danger ahead.

Without warning, the swell of the waves caught the excursion boat and plunged it directly in front of the hull of the large ore boat. The hull of the ore boat collided amidships of the excursion boat on the starboard side. The impact caused passengers outside the enclosed decks to be plunged overboard into the icy water. The crunch of steel against steel as the two vessels collided sounded like the grinding of metal through a diamond saw blade. Sparks flew. Several women screamed with voices louder than the high waves thrashing the ships. Couples clung to one another as they fell into the water. Others were calling out to their mates after being separated by the impact. Those inside the enclosed parts of the excursion boat began opening the sliding windows and instinctively jumped into the water. The impact pushed in the starboard side of the excursion boat about four feet, and water gushed into the boat as wave after wave lashed at it. The huge ore boat came to a complete stop and now lay dead in the water with its full cargo.

The force of the impact also tossed Julie, Brad, John and Elaine into the water. Each went under the water and then bobbed to the surface. They looked around for each other and began calling out each other's names.

At the time of its construction the hull of the excursion boat had been built so that it had a number of separate air chambers that could be opened and closed from the wheel house of the excursion boat. Once a collision appeared to be imminent, the young captain pulled the switch that closed the various compartments of the hull. Although the impact made a substantial gap in the starboard side of the boat and some water had entered the hull, the air chambers were left intact and they were able to keep it afloat. It tilted slightly from having taken in some water, but those passengers still aboard were told by the crew to stay aboard but to go to the port side of the boat for their own safety.

The impact had damaged one of the diesel fuel compartments in the hull, causing some of the fuel to empty into the water. The wind continued to blow with more intensity, propelling the tour boat back toward the hull of the huge ore boat. Crew members still on the excursion boat used megaphones to warn passengers who had fallen into the water to get away from the boats.

The clouds continued to darken the sky and seemed to close in on the surface of the water. Because the list of the excursion boat had somewhat subsided, the passengers remaining on board were able to upright some chairs and find places in the enclosures to either sit or stand.

The loudspeaker informed the passengers that the boat was safe, despite its list, and that the bulkheads between the compartments were closed so that the boat would remain intact. The pandemonium and confusion of the passengers subsided as the captain assured them they were all right. Although some inside the enclosures had fallen or bumped the steel sides of the enclosures, the crew was able to render first aid to them. Some passengers were complaining of sore arms and legs from falling; others were suffering from bruised faces, but the overall assessment was that no one had been seriously injured.

Almost fifty passengers, including Julie, Brad and the Larimores, were in the water. All the women who were hurled into the water had life preservers, but some of the men had not taken such precautions and were now calling for help to those still on board. They were bobbing up and down with the waves and waving their arms for help. Panic and fear showed on their faces.

Julie and Brad were separated as they were projected into the water. When Brad surfaced, all he could see were the faces of other passengers as he scanned the water for Julie. With a round life preserver for support, he started swimming among the passengers as the waves crested up and down.

On the starboard side near the bow of the huge ore boat the crew lowered two lifeboats from their davits with three crewmen in each boat. About the same time Jay Hammond, aboard a 41 foot Coast Guard cutter with a crew of six, sped toward the disaster. Following the cutter was another cutter of like size and also the 180-foot Mondew cutter. The front cutter was closing on the disaster scene at full speed and its crew was in readiness to rescue those in the water.

Julie had never learned to swim and had earlier mentioned her fear of water to Brad. Although her life jacket supported her in the water, the waves kept washing over her, causing her to swallow water and her body to be swept from side to side and even to be dunked under occasionally.

Brad continued to swim among the victims calling out Julie's name. The water was cold and he had to find Julie. Suddenly he heard her voice.

"Brad, Brad!! Help me, help me!"

Brad searched the water but did not see Julie. He was

frightened. Then he saw her face and dark hair bouncing among the waves. He heard her call his name and darted toward her and put his arms around her. He wiped her hair off her face and tried to help her ride with the waves to prevent her swallowing more water. Julie was shivering and crying. Then she smiled when Brad touched her.

Brad looked around and saw the Coast Guard cutter approaching and nearing the bobbing passengers who tried to maneuver themselves toward the cutter. Its crew lowered some dinghies, and the crewmen started to pull people into the dinghies. At about the same time, the lifeboats from the huge ore boat were placed in the water and their crews helped the wet and frightened people into the lifeboats. Julie was breathless and bewildered as Brad tried to comfort her.

"Hold on, Julie. We'll be helped into the boat any minute now."

The waves kept pushing the excursion boat into the people in the water, and the captain was helpless to control it. The crew of the second cutter, which arrived almost simultaneously on the scene, was maneuvering the cutter near the excursion boat and uncurling lines to throw to the crew. The crew picked up the lines and fastened them around the cutter's cleats so the boat could be towed. Meanwhile, Brad had maneuvered Julie up beyond the dinghy to the side of the cutter where Jay Hammond and some of his crew had put a safety ladder over the side. Brad told Julie to grab the rung of the ladder as Jay Hammond leaned over the side to help her. Brad tried to lift her up the ladder.

As the Mondew arrived at the disaster scene, its crew took over the lines hooked onto the excursion boat to help pull the boat farther from the victims. The passengers floating near the lifeboats lowered from the ore boat were being helped into these lifeboats and were quickly wrapped in blankets.

When filled with passengers, the lifeboats proceeded towards the 180-foot Mondew. The drenched passengers were taken below deck and wrapped in blankets while crew members of the ore boat continued to work with stealth and speed to get the people out of the cold water.

The Mondew's cabin quarters were ample for the care of the rescued passengers. Some of the rescued were led to the crew's quarters; others collapsed to the floor and chose to occupy the galley and eating quarters.

Jay Hammond and his crew walked among the passengers trying to comfort those who appeared to be in shock and administered first aid to those needing attention. Blankets were given to the women, and hot chocolate and coffee were handed out from the galley.

Brad and John made sure Julie and Elaine, huddled together in the corner of the cabin, were safe stiting on the floor. They then proceeded to help passengers from the lifeboats onto the Mondew. The diesel motors of the boat were kept idling while the passengers were being helped onto the vessel so that some warm air could be switched on to provide heat for the chilled and chattering passengers.

A tugboat arrived on the scene to tow the disabled excursion boat back to its port. The lines which attached the excursion boat to the cleats of the cutter were now thrown over to the tugboat to enable it to start towing.

Brad and John had assisted the crew of the Mondew in rescuing the wet and fearful passengers and in getting them comfortable in the boat's large cabin. They helped some crew members distribute warm drinks to the victims. They then huddled down next to Julie and Elaine, with Brad putting both his arms around Julie and holding her close.

"Were you scared?"

"Oh, Brad, I've never learned how to swim, and I couldn't find you. I was afraid something had happened to you," she confided through chattering teeth and blue lips.

"Julie, thank goodness we found each other, and I have you back in my arms. I don't know what I'd do if something happened to you. You mean so much to me."

"Brad, I know, and today I realized just how much you mean to me, too."

Jay Hammond radioed ahead to have warm blankets ready when he docked. He also alerted taxicabs and buses to be ready to transfer the passengers to their homes, hotels or motels. As the Mondew glided into its slip at the Coast Guard station, crew members stood ready to let down the gangplank to permit the passengers to depart to the waiting busses and taxicabs on the wharf.

Brad helped Julie to her feet and made sure she was adequately covered by her blanket before they disembarked. Following the Larimores and other passengers from the vessel, Julie and Brad walked to a waiting taxicab with the Larimores. Brad stopped, however and looked for Jay Hammond who was standing at the base of the gangplank assisting passengers onto the wharf. Brad shook Jay's hand and thanked him for the rescue service. He then joined Julie in the taxi and asked to be driven to the hotel.

As the cab pulled up in front of the hotel, other cabs and busses were already beginning to discharge passengers from the ill-fated excursion cruise. Upon entering the lobby of the hotel, they saw Ben talking to several people who were attending the convention. Ben saw them enter the lobby.

"My goodness. What happened?"

"We were in an accident. Julie, the Larimores and I, along with a number of other passengers, were thrown from the tour boat into the waters near the Disciple Islands. Except for a few bruised and wet passengers, I think all passengers survived the collision."

Brad suggested they go up to his room where they

could arrange to get their clothes dried out and to change into some dry garments.

Brad phoned the Larimores' room and talked to Elaine about lending Julie some clothes for the drive back home. Brad offered Julie his room while he went to the Larimores' to get her some dry clothes.

He returned with several pieces of clothing draped over his arm as he knocked on the door.

"Julie, I'm handing in the clothes from Elaine. Why don't you jump in the shower, change and I'll wait for you."

Julie emerged from the bathroom in her borrowed clothes, holding her wet clothes in one hand and the large towel wrapped around her head with the other hand. Brad looked for a laundry bag and, finding none, phoned housekeeping for a plastic bag in which to put Julie's things.

"I'd like to drive up this weekend to see you. Will you be free?"

" Oh, I'd like that. It's not my weekend to work. Brad, that would be great."

"I'll stay at the motel. How about 4 p.m. next Saturday?"

"I'll fix dinner and we can watch some TV later on. There are some great country singers on TV on Saturday night."

A knock at the door interrupted their conversation. A hotel maid had arrived and offered Brad a plastic laundry bag. He tipped her generously and then began to help Julie put the wet clothes in the bag.

"We'd better think about finding Ben, Julie." He was already waiting for them in the lobby when they arrived.

Brad walked out to the car with them feeling already a bit lost without Julie.

"I'll see you Saturday," as he waved good-bye.

Shortly into their travels, Ben turned to Julie.

"That was quite an experience you had today. I heard all about it while waiting for you. Are you okay?"

"Yes, but it was scary. I couldn't find Brad for a while. I kept getting dunked under the water with every wave, and it was cold, and it seemed like I shouted forever to find him before he came swimming toward me."

"Were you at least having fun before the accident?"

"Oh, yes. I do enjoy being with him. We have such a good time when we're together and I find myself missing him when he's not around."

"He seems like a fine young man. I'm glad things are going well for you two. Now, why don't you relax the rest of the way back."

"Thanks, Ben." She crossed her arms and closed her eyes. She thought about Chrissy and wondered how she and the sitter had fared during her absence. She smiled when she thought of opening her arms for Chrissy to run into them. She would feel content when she would walk into her home. Then her thoughts changed to the four days she had spent with Brad. She thought about what he said to her, the way he respected her, about the places they had been together and about her feelings toward him.

Ben made a right turn and then a left one which jolted her from her day dreaming. She looked around to get her bearings and then went back to her reverie.

"He told me he loves me," as she smiled in remembrance of the moment. Suddenly her thoughts turned to her age and she wondered how old Brad might be. Their age difference had not crossed her mind before.

"I wonder how old he really is," she quietly pondered. As for her, she had just turned twenty-three. She began some mental math.

"Let's see. He's gone to law school and has been in the Air Force Reserves for three or four years. He could be nearly thirty."

She sat up in the car seat a little and opened her eyes. "Shouldn't we be home pretty soon?"

"Yes, just a few more miles." The car was quiet the rest of the way back to their hometown. They arrived shortly after dinnertime and went their separate ways after Ben dropped Julie off at her home.

Julie turned the knob on her front door. "I'm home." Both Chrissy and the sitter bounced from the kitchen and Chrissy ran to her mother who had bent down to catch her in her arms. The sitter told Julie everything had gone just fine. Julie spent the evening with Chrissy but did not mention the accident to her for fear of upsetting her. Once Chrissy went to bed, Julie unpacked. She sat in a sofa chair, stretched her legs and thought again about Brad. Saturday he would visit her. How she was looking forward to being with him again.

Julie drew her legs up against her chest and snuggled herself into a corner of the chair.

"It's good to be home," she said aloud for no one but herself to hear. A strong sense of security and contentment settled over her. Then her mind raced with thoughts of Brad again. She thought about his living in Minneapolis and a lawyer there; she compared what her life in a big city might be with that in her home town.

"I'm so fond of him; perhaps too much. I should talk to my mom and Carol about it tomorrow."

She sauntered off to bed and fell asleep with a slight smile on her face.

## Chapter 10

THE LAST WEEK IN JUNE ARRIVED. Brad drove up to Milaca in the afternoon, checked into the motel, changed into comfortable clothes and then headed to Julie's. Brad was hoping to talk with Julie about his feelings toward her. Maybe, he thought, she might do the same.

As Brad entered the house, he greeted Julie and Chrissy, remarking that the trip from the Cities was relaxing and enjoyable.

"I'm so glad I didn't pull duty at the Reserves this weekend. I'd much rather spend this time with you."

Julie had dressed in a white blouse and blue skirt with low-heeled navy shoes. Her dark hair fell shoulder length making a beautiful contrast against her white blouse.

The three of them decided to walk around the yard looking at the flowers. When they walked over to Julie's small garden, she knelt down to view her tomato plants which were climbing their support sticks. There were rows of carrots, beans, onions and peas which already had two months growth to them. She explained that it was still too early to pull some of the vegetables for a dinner meal.

Brad praised Julie's care of her flowers and garden. His amazement at her prowess in such activities showed on his face as he complimented her. The small tomatoes and the green vegetables growing in the rich black dirt were a sight.

"Seeing this beautiful garden has made me hungry. Should we think about dinner?"

Brad put his right arm under Julie's and took Chrissy by the hand as they walked back into the house through the back door. Julie headed for the kitchen to start dinner while Brad walked into the living room and turned on the television to watch the news. Chrissy decided to go back out to the yard to play on her swing set until dinner.

The au gratin potatoes were put into the oven to bake after Julie had prepared the stuff-baked pork chops and had placed them in the oven on the rack below the potatoes for about an hour. She had placed a tray of cauliflower, broccoli, and carrots with cheese sauce back in the refrigerator to keep cool until she was ready to microwave them.

"Brad, want a drink?"

"A beer would be nice."

Julie handed Brad a can of beer and a glass, and sat down in a chair opposite him and opened a beer for herself.

"You've mentioned several times that you're in the Air Force Reserves. Where are you stationed? How often do you go?"

"I am stationed at the base near the airport in the Cities. I spend one week end each month on duty and two weeks each summer to Reserve duty. I'm a navigator on a C-130 four-engine turbo-prop transport airplane."

"How long have you been doing this?"

"Four years now. I applied during the summer after my last year in law school and trained after I graduated. I hope to continue on indefinitely."

Julie excused herself to check on dinner. She called Chrissy in and invited Brad to the table in the cove between the living room and kitchen. They chatted casually about the convention in Duluth. When the collision of the tour boat and ore boat came up, Chrissy asked with childlike concern,

"Were you hurt, mom?"

"No, honey. Brad helped me out of the water."

Brad caught the look on Julie's face and deflected anymore conversation about the mishap by changing the subject.

"Julie, you're a great cook," and with that offered to help Julie by drying the dishes. He asked about the absence of a dishwasher. She said that when her little house was built, the kitchens apparently were not built for installations of dishwashers. He gave her a friendly little nudge while they were standing next to each other at the sink. Julie grinned.

Chrissy scampered out the door into the yard once she saw dishes were done. Brad sat down on the sofa and asked Julie if she would join him.

"You know, Julie, I wanted to visit you this weekend because I was hoping we could talk about us."

"What do you mean, Brad?"

Brad took Julie's hand in his.

"Julie, I'm in love with you and have been since the first time I saw you at the law school seminars. I didn't know who you were until I saw you again in the little cafe, but I know now that you're the one I've been looking for."

A half smile crossed Julie's face, but she seemed otherwise unmoved by what he was saying. The only thing she could think of saying was a rather feeble "Really?"

"I've tried to show you that I love you and respect you whenever we've been together. I hope you know I would never treat you with anything but love and respect."

Julie heard her daughter running toward the back door of the house.

"Here comes Chrissy."

Brad sat back, released Julie's hand and asked Chrissy if she had a good time in the yard.

"Uh, huh," she affirmed as she climbed up on Julie's lap. Brad knew the moment was lost so he suggested the three of them go for a walk down the block.

"That sounds like a good idea. What d'ya say, Chrissy. Are you up for a little exercise?"

Brad opened the front door and with Julie holding Chrissy's hand, the three started toward downtown. Occasionally, Julie would cast a backward look toward her home. They talked about the green lawns, the tall trees, and maintenance of flowers and gardens along the way.

"Mom, I'm getting tired."

Julie and Brad both looked at one another.

"Well, maybe it's time we turn around and get this little girl home," Brad offered lovingly.

Once home, Chrissy got a second wind. She ran to her room and retrieved a game which she laid out on the kitchen table, asking Brad if he would play the game with her. Julie suggested they make it a threesome. Halfway through, however, Chrissy started yawning.

"Time for bed, Chrissy. Come on. I'll tuck you in."

Julie snuggled Chrissy into her quilts, turned off the light and returned to the living room.

"Julie, come sit next to me."

Without answering, Julie sat down beside Brad on the sofa.

"Remember the walk we took downtown while at the convention and we looked into the window of a jewelry store?"

"Sure. Weren't some of those pieces beautiful?"

"Yes they were. Julie, I'd like to get you the one I thought you had your eye on."

"But why, Brad? You shouldn't do that."

"Julie," Brad put his hand on Julie's, "I've been a bachelor for a lot of years, but when I saw you, that was it. I'm in love with you. What else can I say?"

"Brad, I'm very fond of you. I love being with you, but there's this feeling I have which is hard to explain. Maybe it's because of my failed marriage."

Brad looked at Julie, put his arm around her, and pulled her closer to him. Julie moved toward him and felt the comfort of his arm around her. He remained silent while Julie talked on.

"You know, Brad, that my feelings were very badly hurt by my last marriage and the divorce left me with a terrible distrust of men generally. I felt completely betrayed by my first husband."

"Julie, look at me. Have I done anything to create those kinds of feelings toward me?"

"Brad, you've been incredibly good to me and I care for you, but we need to be honest here. Would I fit into your group of friends? Besides, I don't think I would be happy in a big city away from my relatives and friends. I'm a small town girl and the thought of leaving here really bothers me."

"But I would do everything to make you happy and you could see your friends and relatives as often as you wanted. Are you sure those are the real reasons?"

Julie's thoughts turned to her first marriage. It didn't last. It ended in divorce and left her alone and devastated.

"Brad, I've had a dream of starting my own antique business. I really want to achieve that dream. I've even been saving my money toward making it happen."

"That's great, Julie. I could help you to satisfy that dream. Nothing would give me more pleasure or satisfaction."

"Thanks, Brad. I know you mean that, but it's something I want to do on my own, something that will help me feel I am a success."

"I'm proud of you, Julie. Helping you with this would not make me any less proud of you."

"But you don't understand. I've got to do it myself. I've studied books on beginning a business and I'm doing research on managing a business. This means a lot to me."

"If you don't want me to interfere, I can understand your ambition to do this alone."

They sat for a long time together, his arm around her, her head on his shoulder. Occasionally he'd run his hand through her hair and pull her closer to him. They both closed their eyes and sat until Brad broke the silence.

"Julie, I'll always want to be with you, to protect you and care for you. Will you marry me?"

"I know you will, Brad. But but I just can't right now."

Brad was bewildered. He had told Julie how he felt about her; he had told her he was in love with her but she was not receptive to his pleading. He told her he would always love her.

"I'm sorry, Brad. It's just me. It's the way I am."

"I'm trying to understand, Julie, but I'll never give you up."

Brad looked at his watch. It was getting late and he decided he should return to the motel. She asked if he planned to stop by the next day before he left.

"Yes, of course. I'd like to take a minute to say hello to your neighbor, Ben, if that's alright."

Julie moved closer to Brad. She put her arms around him and kissed him goodnight.

"You'll phone me, won't you?"

When she dropped her arms, Brad moved toward the door to leave. He was obviously discouraged but said gently and kindly, "I'll phone you every week."

Brad arrived the following morning at 10 a.m. He had phoned Ben from the motel and asked him if he could stop for a short visit before leaving to drive back to the Cities. Fearing that Ben might say something about their relationship, Julie was hesitant when Brad asked her if she and Chrissy wanted to join him at Ben's. Brad sensed her hesitation and then suggested he would make the visit alone. He said good-bye and drove across the street to Ben's.

"How have you been?" Ben greeted as he offered Brad a chair. "Did you enjoy your visit with Julie?"

"It was fine."

From Brad's expression, however, Ben suspected that the visit turned out to the contrary and couldn't resist pressing the issue.

"Is something wrong?"

"Not exactly."

Such a remark concerned Ben for he had the feeling that Brad had fallen in love with Julie and that the visit did not turn out on the high side for Brad.

Ben had been a neighbor of Julie's for about five years, knew what marital and other problems she had been through, and sensed through snippets of conversation with her that she was going through a conflict of desires and passions. At times she seemed embittered by her past experiences and also seemed unable to control the direction of her thoughts about what way of life should make her the happiest. Ben was certain she was still concerned about her marriage. Such thinking was understandable to him.

Ben changed the discussion to law and upcoming trials in court, and neither tried to reopen the discussion about Julie. They closed their visit with further talk about the past convention and the boat accident and an agreement to get together again sometime.

Brad had a full schedule in trials of civil cases for the ensuing months but his mind, when free to wander, always settled on thoughts of Julie. He phoned her within the week.

"I want to visit you, again, Julie. I miss you."

Delighted, Julie told him to drive up and she'd be waiting for him.

As he stood on her doorstep the next day, he couldn't contain his excitement.

"Julie, let's drive over to a nearby town and find some quaint little cafe where we can eat and talk."

"We could go to Ogilvie. It's a few miles east of here. I know a nice little supper club that has good food and a quiet atmosphere just right for talking."

At the cafe they found the most private of the booths. Brad extended his hand across the table and placed it gingerly on Julie's.

"I'd love to drive up more often but most of my weekends are taken by trial preparation or my commitment to the Reserves. I wish I could find a way to spend more time with you."

"I think of you every day, about the cruise together, our meeting at the summer convention. Yes, it would be nice to have more time for one another."

"So, how are your plans coming for an antique business?"

"Well, slow but steady, really. I'm still saving my money so I can have enough to buy a few antiques to start out. I probably will try to do it part-time in the beginning."

"Julie, do you know how proud I am of you?"

Her smile spoke volumes to him.

*Chapter 11*

AT ONE OF THE FALL weekend Reserves meetings, Brad realized that more and more meetings were being held about the situation in the Middle East and that some personnel were being activated for duty in Britain and in Europe. He began to follow closely the news about Iraq's demands on Kuwait during the summer of 1990. He read about Iraq's claim of the overproduction of crude oil by Kuwait, and that Kuwait was drilling some of its oil wells on the slant and taking oil from the Iraqi oil fields. He also read about Iraq's demands for rights to lease some islands off the coast of Kuwait for Iraqi shipping, because of the damage to Iraq's own ports in the Iraq-Iran war.

On September 27, 1990, the news came that the Emir of Kuwait had addressed the UN General Assembly. The United Nations passed a number of resolutions directing that Iraq leave Kuwait and withdraw to within its own borders. Similar announcements were made by the heads of other nations.

Brad's concern over these events prompted him to

report to the Reserve base weekly to ascertain the status of the activity in connection with the Middle East crisis. A few days after Christmas, Brad received a letter from headquarters that announced certain officers would be taken to complement some C-130 Hercules airlift planes to be assigned to a base in the vicinity of the Persian Gulf. He contacted his law firm and requested leave with the understanding in writing that Brad would be able to return to the law firm following his release from active duty. Brad had participated as a navigator on the C-130s on special air support operations previously. Those air support operations had been confined to the continental United States with one flight to Central America on a medical and food supply mission.

On January 3, 1991, Brad, as navigator of one of the C-130 Hercules, felt the wheels of the huge plane touch the runway of the landing strip near his reserve base after completing a four-hour military mission in the states. As he emerged from the airplane, he was met by the chief navigator while on his way into the airlift group building.

"Brad, pack your bags. You're leaving later today on assignment to the Persian Gulf."

He went home, phoned his folks, and explained that he was flying out that evening. Then he phoned Julie and told her of his assignment.

"I love you, Julie. I'll write when I reach base and whenever else I can."

"But where will you be?"

"I honestly don't know yet."

"Please be careful, Brad. Take good care of yourself."

"You, too. Good-bye, Julie."

Julie slowly placed the receiver back on its hook, mumbling aloud to herself. "Brad's gone. My God, what if he doesn't come back? What if these last months were all just a dream?" She went to bed early that night, but she didn't sleep well.

He flew commercially to Detroit where he reported to the Selfridges National Guard Air Base and quartered overnight. The following morning he was assigned to a Tactical Air Lift Squadron in which he would be performing the duties of a Navigator on a C-130 Hercules, to be stationed at an air base in the desert in Saudi Arabia.

His orders for duty provided for a flight overseas on a C-5 Galaxy Transport plane with thirty-nine other Air Force Reserve personnel from other bases who were also assigned to the Persian Gulf area. The transport plane landed in Madrid, Spain, for refueling before completing the flight to Jubal, Saudi Arabia. The trip took twenty hours overall. Once at Jubal, Brad boarded a C-130 Hercules bound for Shartjah in the United Arab Emirates where he was to be based temporarily. There he was quartered in an air conditioned tent with complete toilet and shower facilities. The land beyond the base was desert, and for miles there was nothing but sand, which blew into everything on the base.

A tactics shop had been set up in a large tent at the temporary base at which Brad was ordered to a briefing session the next day on a C-130 Hercules plane under C-130 Tasking Orders. He was instructed as to the activity in which the planes would participate in the Persian Gulf and how the activity was to be performed.

Once briefed, her returned to his quarters. All he could think about was Julie and the uncertainty of his life at this moment.

January 6, 1991

Dear Julie,

I'm writing from a base I'm currently assigned to in a tactical Air Force Group near the Persian Gulf. When I was told I was to be assigned, I got my gear together, grabbed a plane for Detroit where I got my orders and was assigned to this Airlift Group. I've been busy this past fall and winter so far with primarily my work with the law firm. Now I'm devoting all my time to my duties here. I don't know how long I'll be over here, but I've been assured I can return to the law firm if and when my status here changes.

I sure have missed seeing you since this past summer, but I take some comfort from thinking about our good times together. I miss you. I am in love with you and dream about you. This will never change. I have some pictures of you and me on the stern of the Caribbean cruise boat I brought along. I've looked at them constantly since I left the states.

Here's my present military address. Please write.

If I'm assigned new duties at another address I'll be sure to send you the new address.

All my love,

Brad

Julie received the letter more than a week later when she arrived at home from work. She ripped it open and read it several times, put it back in the envelope and placed it in her top dresser drawer. She knew she had grown incredibly fond of Brad and enjoyed being with him when they had been together, but she still felt uncertain about their future together. It was something she thought about continually and discussed often with her friend Carol. Carol and Julie met frequently and had talked often about their love lives, or the lack of them, with each other. Shortly after Brad had left for the cities following his last visit with Julie, she phoned Carol and asked her to come over. They sat down on the sofa together and after some mundane conversation Carol got to the heart of things.

"What's with Brad?"

"It's just that sometimes I'm not sure how I feel about him."

"Why?"

"That's the problem. Actually I'm not sure why."

"Well, you like him, don't ya?"

"Of course I do. And he told me he loves me and he even wanted to get a ring for me that we saw in a jewelry store window in Duluth."

"So, what's the problem? Aren't you sure about him?"

"Well, I keep on thinking about my marriage and divorce and I have to wonder if I even know what love means. Maybe my former marriage was only infatuation?"

"Do you think of him as just a friend or do you have deep feelings about him?"

"That's the problem."

"Do you miss him when he's not with you?"

"Yes, I do, sometimes, well, most times. Actually, almost all the time."

"There you go."

"But he lives in Minneapolis and practices law there. All my friends, you especially, and my mom and sister live here. I don't want to leave here."

"What makes you think you have to live in Minneapolis? You'd probably live in a suburb or maybe he'd change his law practice to Milaca."

"Carol, he was born and brought up in Minneapolis. His family lives in a suburb, and his friends are there."

"So, there are a lot of unanswered questions, huh?"
"I suppose so; the uncertainty bothers me."
"But you have that feeling for him?"
"Uh, huh. I think I'm in love with him."

## Chapter 12

ON JANUARY 17, 1991, while Brad was still asleep in his quarters, he was abrasively awakened by a fellow airman who announced that the war had just officially begun. From Brad's airlift group, a crew consisting of a pilot, co-pilot, engineer, two load masters, and himself as navigator were assigned to a particular C-130 Hercules plane to airlift troops and equipment from positions in lower Saudi Arabia to a northern position along the Saudi Arabia-Iraq border. The C-130 and crew moved airborne troops and equipment around the clock for a three-week stretch and awaited further orders for possible medical air evacuation.

The landing strips were made by bulldozers which had been airlifted to the northern-most position near the border with the landing strips carved out of the desert mounds and sand. They were rolled and constantly kept leveled with graders and other equipment.

Once the war started, the Iraqis began using Scud missiles aimed for the major cities and military bases in Saudi Arabia. Near King Khalid City, about 30 miles from the Iraqi border, but still in Saudi Arabia, a large military base was maintained by the American forces. Brad's duties took him to this large base quite often. The personnel at this base were usually quartered in tents with eleven men to a tent and an outhouse for each tent. A portable showering facility was set up which consisted of a wooden scaffolding that supported a medium-size tank with a spray nozzle.

Also based at this military city were water trucks which were operated by personnel assigned to water purification units that supplied the water used for showering and drinking purposes. Trucks were also used to carry military personnel into Iraq to build prisoner of war camps for captured Iraqi soldiers.

The temperatures ranged from 95 to 115 degrees Fahrenheit until about the middle of December, when the weather dropped below freezing and it rained.

The large army tanks in the transportation units had difficulty moving about in the rainy season because of the mud that developed. The cold and rain lasted until sometime into February when it became warm again.

The military city that was identified as KKMC had a large airfield located near it. Apparently the Iraqis were attempting to damage this airfield for in the late hours almost every afternoon, sirens would signal a warning of incoming Scuds through the air. The Scuds would come in toward the base at a height of about 10,000 feet. As they approached KKMC, they would be met by Patriot missiles from five Patriot batteries surrounding the air base. The missiles from the Patriot batteries were deployed simultaneously in order to converge on the Scuds at the same time and destroy them.

## Chapter 13

JULIE AND CAROL CONTINUED to see each other almost daily with Carol usually visiting at Julie's home each afternoon. During one of the get-togethers, Carol suggested they should get a sitter for Chrissy and attend a nightclub at the edge of town one evening.

"The club has a quite a good reputation for getting good bands."

"I like its dining area and the way the horseshoe bar is separated from the dining part and the food is great. Besides, there's a small dance floor in front of the band stand."

Julie offered her own assessment, "I love the soft leather upholstered chairs in the lounge. And, hey, if there's no band, we'll just play the jukebox."

Julie had been to the club before with other friends, knew one of the bartenders, and always enjoyed the evening with Carol and other friends in the club's familiar surroundings. Neither of the girls, both raised to be quite proper and respectable young women, paid any attention to strangers or gentlemen who were too pushy except upon an introduction by someone they knew.

Their evenings out together proved so enjoyable that they had decided to socialize at least once a week.

In preparation for their latest outing, Carol came to Julie's armed with the daily newspaper from a community about a half-hour away from Milaca. This larger community had a better selection of nightclubs at which more celebrity bands performed nightly. Country music was the preference of the listening and dancing audiences. Julie and Carol enjoyed country music and after going over the ad, they decided to attend an evening performance of the Jayhawks, a country group playing at the Blue Owl Nightclub.

The group was on a tour from its home base in a western state on its way to Nashville where it would be competing in a contest for bands and singers. The tour provided them with a source of income to cover the expenses of the group and their traveling bus which had sleeping quarters and a galley. The girls decided to check out the band that Wednesday evening.

Even before they entered the club, the women were virtually bombarded with the loud strains of country music. They walked past the side of the bandstand toward a table near the small stage. The club seated about 125 patrons and was filled to capacity tonight. It had a small teakwood dance floor in front of the stage and scenic murals of the surrounding habitat on the walls. Speakers were spaced about the interior and the music reverberated from wall to wall and bounced off the purple painted ceiling.

Julie and Carol ordered beer from the waitress and began a conversation about the band and its members with her. The women agreed that the drummer and piano player were good looking. Carol noticed the drummer watching her, and Julie caught the piano player casting an occasional glance her way. When the waitress brought their beers to the table, Carol asked her if she knew the musicians.

"Uh, huh. The drummer's name is Jerry Cramer. He must be about six feet, don't you think. And he's sure easy on the eyes, that dark hair and all, huh? Listen, I'll tell you more later."

She returned about thirty minutes later.

"The piano player and lead singer of the band is Steve Palmer. I kind of tease him about the fact that the drummer is a few inches taller than him and that he looks just like a little boy with all that wavy blonde hair."

With that comment, she proceeded to wait on the other tables around them.

Sylvester, manager of the club, stopped at the tables and booths to greet his customers and to ask if the service was okay. When he stopped at Julie and Carol's table they asked him how the band happened to be booked at his nightclub. He informed them that the band leader had told him that he had heard about a country western band contest in Nashville and had contacted him earlier for a booking on the way there. The band felt they had reached a leveling stage of performance in their home state, had the confidence to compete with the same format bands in the country western music field and should do well in the contest. To pay for expenses incurred en route, they booked in cities along their itinerary to Nashville.

During intermission Steve and Jerry walked over to Julie and Carol, introduced themselves, and asked if they could join the girls. The women tried not to look as pleased as they felt. Jerry sat down next to Carol and asked if she was enjoying the music. Steve sat down next to Julie and asked how the girls happened to be out for the evening.

"You guys are really good. Where you from?" ventured Carol.

Jerry went through an explanation about the band being from a small town in a nearby state and that they were en route to the contest of country music bands.

Steve noticed immediately that Julie was not wearing a wedding band and asked her where she was from. Julie responded that both she and Carol were long-time friends and that both of them were from Milaca, about 30 miles away. Julie thought Steve was a good-looking man, and was interested in chatting with him. Carol and Jerry seemed taken with each other during the 15-minute intermission. As the men prepared to go back on stage, Jerry suggested to Carol that they remain after the performance, then join the band in their bus parked outside the nightclub.

"We'll see. We'll let you know," ventured Carol, with a bit of false timidity.

When the two men returned to the stage to continue the music, Carol asked Julie,

"What do you think about waiting until the show is over and joining them?"

"Boy, I don't know. I don't particularly like the idea. Besides, we'll get home too late."

"They seem to be nice guys and I'd kind of like to get acquainted with Jerry."

"I can't say as I'm necessarily interested in the other guy and I still don't think it's a good idea."

After that, Carol caught Jerry's eyes as he looked their way and nodded her head from side to side indicating "no." Carol leaned over to Julie and again mentioned she was attracted to Jerry and sure would like to see him again.

Julie seemed a bit puzzled by the whole conversation but said, "Well, if it means that much to you."

The two musicians still continued to watch the girls, smiled at them and nodded, signifying they wanted the girls to say "yes."

After the next set, and while those who were dancing to the music were leaving the dance floor, Jerry walked to the girls' table and tried one more time.

"C'mon, you guys. Give me one good reason why you can't stay. Steve and I would like to get to know you better."

Julie questioned him. "How about we sit here in a booth for a few minutes after the band is through? I don't think the management would mind."

"That'd be okay. See you both after we finish playing."

After the final set the patrons slowly made their way to the door and began to leave. Julie and Carol left their table for the nearest booth where they were joined by Jerry and Steve. Jerry sat down next to Carol and Steve next to Julie. The musicians asked the girls if they wanted a beer.

"Just coffee for me," said Julie and Carol nodded an affirmative for herself as well.

Jerry started the conversation. He repeated the information in the newspaper article.

"I suppose you're wondering what brings us here to the Blue Owl? We've had this band since high school and are touring on the way to a contest in Nashville. We'll be playing this gig through Saturday and then move on to a ballroom in Lanesville, Wisconsin, next week. We plan to reach the contest in time to rehearse for a week or so before the contest."

Jerry leaned over the table and in a low voice, as if he were revealing a deep, dark secret, said, "Steve and I are both single but some of the other guys had to leave their wives behind. Being on the road can be tough sometimes. So, where are you girls from?"

Carol took the initiative. "We're both from Milaca, about 30 miles from here."

Steve jumped into the conversation. "Did you come over here just to hear us play?"

Both girls replied that they had.

Then Jerry broke in, "So, you both single?"

He got an answer from Julie, "Sorta. We're both divorced."

Jerry ventured out on the somewhat precarious waters of the conversation.

"I'd like to see you again, Carol, but I don't want you two to have to drive over here again. Could we come up by you tomorrow and visit?"

Carol looked at Julie, then back at Jerry.

"Is that okay with you, Julie?"

Steve quickly added, "I'd sure like to see you again, Julie."

Although Julie didn't feel any particular attraction to Steve, since Brad was now in the Persian Gulf, she didn't see any reason for discouraging the visit. Both the men seemed to be gentlemen. Suddenly, the lights in the nightclub flickered a couple of times which prompted

Julie to say, "We better leave now. We have a solid half-hour drive home yet."

Steve stepped away from the table. "If it works out all right , how about we drive over to see you and Carol tomorrow after rehearsal? How does 3 p.m. sound?"

Both girls agreed that that would be fine, so Steve and Jerry wrote Julie and Carol's addresses on cocktail napkins. When Steve inquired as to which place they should go to, Julie remarked, "Let's meet at my place."

After complimenting them again on their music, Julie and Carol left for home. The drive home was uneventful but filled with discussion about the music and the men.

Carol arrived at Julie's shortly after lunch the next day and found her vacuuming the living room. Carol yelled above the noise that she'd like to help so Julie handed her a dust cloth and polish to use on the bookshelves and tables. Within an hour they had the house looking spic-and-span for the guests.

While in her bedroom sprucing up a bit, Julie pulled out the top dresser drawer and picked up the letter Brad had written her. She sat on the edge of her bed, reread the letter, tenderly placed it back under some lingerie, then viewed herself in her mirror.

"Mirror, mirror. What do you see? Brad is gone and I need company." Impulsively, she decided again to change her usual coiffure by making an arrangement on top of her head that would make her look more mature and sophisticated.

The doorbell rang. There stood Jerry and Steve, each with a six-pack of beer under his arm. Both men commented on the house. The girls invited them into the living room. The men sat on the velour sofa and the girls opposite them in the fabric-covered chairs.

Steve offered the girls a beer, and both accepted. Steve followed Julie into the kitchen to help retrieve some glasses. As the two stood together in the kitchen, Steve again praised Julie on her well-kept and cozy home. He asked how long she had lived there, and followed the question with a bit of small talk. Without expecting it, he suddenly became personal with her.

"Can I ask you what happened to your ex-husband?"

"My ex? He disappeared, so I had to get a lawyer, who located him, and then represented me in my divorce." Julie dropped her eyes as she spoke with a bit of bitterness in her voice and took a step back from Steve.

"Then you live alone with your daughter? Do you have close relatives?"

"I have some family here, And then, of course, there's Carol, and a few close friends. Oh, and my neighbor across the street."

"Which house is his?"

Julie pointed to Ben's house across the street.

"I help him drive to the Cities every so often, mostly to attend legal seminars and conferences, things like that."

Julie hesitated for a moment, and stopped talking for a second or two as Brad flashed into her memory with reminiscing of their good times together. Steve caught her daydreaming and asked if something was wrong. Julie managed a slight smile as she admitted that something had popped into her head for a second but that it was gone now.

While Steve and Julie were talking, Carol and Jerry had become wrapped up in their own conversation. Jerry couldn't seem to get enough information quickly enough and was firing questions at her as fast as she could answer them. Eventually he asked about where she lived and was quick to acknowledge that he'd like to visit her at her place sometime.

"I'd like that, too. Let me know when you'd like to come. I'm usually home after 4:30."

Jerry realized he was becoming quite attracted to Carol and knew he wanted to see her again alone, so he asked her if he could visit her sometime the following day.

Carol found Jerry an unusually likeable person. He was in a successful band and she suspected that the band might even become a national celebrity among the country western bands. She, like Julie, had very little male companionship, primarily because of the smallness of Milaca. Receiving attention from Jerry was not only a nice change of pace from the hum drum of her life, but an extremely pleasant experience.

As Julie and Steve walked from the kitchen, Steve whispered quietly to Julie, "I'm fond of you already."

Julie moved away, suggesting that she and Steve take a ride downtown to pick up some pizza and bread sticks for supper. Her response to Steve's comment was to change the subject and to keep her feelings to herself. She was impressed by Steve's kindness toward her. She told Carol and Jerry that she and Steve were running out to get some pizza. When they returned, they found Jerry with his arm around Carol, the two seemingly quite comfortable with one another on the sofa.

The dinner conversation became more animated when the talk centered on the tour of the band and its appearance at the country music contest. They would be on the tour another two weeks before reaching Nashville for the contest. Jerry looked at Steve.

"We have three more nights at the Blue Owl before we leave for our next stop. I have the rental car until this weekend so I plan on visiting Carol at her place tomorrow afternoon. Do you want to ride over with me and visit Julie?"

Carol smiled broadly when Jerry spoke about visiting her. She was already quite captivated with him. Perhaps she would have a chance to escape her loneliness with this relationship. Had she met a man who could care for her? She hoped Steve had fallen for Julie and wanted to continue to see her. As if Steve read her mind, he turned to Julie.

"I'd like to see you tomorrow if that's okay with you. Jerry can drop me off on the way to Carol's."

Julie saw no harm in letting Steve come over again.

"I don't see why not. I'll make some lasagna so we can eat in."

Jerry dropped Steve off at Julie's house Friday and went on his way to Carol's, but not before he yelled from that car that he would pick him up about 7:30 p.m. so they could get back to the club by 9 p.m.

Steve had brought another six pack of beer and said hello to Chrissy, who was playing in the yard, as he headed for the front door. Julie invited him in and went to check on the lasagna. She still had on her apron so she excused herself and walked into the bedroom, closed the door and changed. When she returned, she was wearing her purple sweater and matching slacks with beige pumps. As she walked into the living room and past the sofa where Steve was sitting, he looked up from a magazine.

"Wow! You look beautiful."

Julie did look attractive with her dark hair, heart-shaped earrings and luminous skin. Steve walked into the kitchen to place the beer in the refrigerator, removed one for himself and handed one to Julie. As they walked back into the living room, Julie headed for the single stuffed lounge chair while Steve plopped himself back on the sofa.

"You know, Julie, when I first saw you at the club the other night, I couldn't take my eyes off you. Girl, you've done something to me."

"Steve, you're just lonesome now. You've been on tour and away from family and friends. Once you get through the contest and get back home, you'll feel differently."

"Sure, I've met other girls but I've never felt about them as I do you. I didn't think before that I knew what love is, but now I seem to be quite sure that is what I feel about you."

Julie shifted uncomfortably in the sofa chair.

"This is rather sudden, isn't it? I don't even know you. I'm sure you're a fine person and you're good looking, so you shouldn't have any trouble meeting women. You know I've been divorced so I question going into another romance. I like you. You seem like a great guy, but I'm pretty content with the way things are for now."

"But, Julie, I'm serious about you. I know I could make you happy and we would have a good life with the income from the band, plus possibly getting into the record business. The band's been well received everywhere we've played."

Steve walked to the chair, leaned over, put his hands on her shoulders and kissed her on the forehead. Julie responded reluctantly when he lifted her out of the chair to stand on the floor and embrace her. He again kissed her on the forehead, then tried to kiss her on the mouth, but she turned her head and said nothing. The kiss fell on her cheek.

"Julie, I'd like to have you and Chrissy join me in Nashville. We need to stay there at least a week rehearsing and preparing for the contest. There's lot of recording studios there, and we might cut an album. Julie, I want to get into the national picture with my band, and I want you by my side as I try to do it."

"But I just can't pick up and leave. I have my home, my friends, my work and family here."

"Look. I'll find a nice cozy place in Nashville for you and your daughter so that I can be with you. This is a dream you can share with me. Please think it over. I want to see you again tomorrow before our last night at the Blue Owl."

Julie removed herself from his arms and went to the kitchen. She had prepared a hot dish of lasagna, and baked an apple pie for dessert. Chrissy joined them for the hour-long meal. Steve fidgeted with his watch and then finally looked at it. He calculated that he could visit another half hour before Jerry would pick him up to go back to the club for their next-to-last performance there.

Early Saturday morning, Carol knocked on Julie's door and walked in exclaiming,

"Last night Jerry asked me to join him when he

arrives in Nashville in a couple of weeks. He says he's fallen in love with me and wants to marry me. I'm so excited I can hardly stand it! I've really fallen for him, too. I told him I'd join him."

"Are you sure you want to do this? Are you certain you're in love with him? Don't make another mistake."

"I think I fell for Jerry the first night we were at the Blue Owl, but I wasn't certain until I saw him yesterday."

Julie was hesitant about telling Carol how she felt about leaving Milaca. Still, she had always been honest with Carol, and now would be no exception. They were, after all, best friends. She admitted would be pretty much alone again with Carol gone, except for some of her family around. Julie wanted to talk about Jerry and Steve, but Carol burst back into conversation with genuine sincerity.

"Look, Julie. You and I have been close friends since early during our high school years."

"I know, Carol. And it's meant a lot to me."

Carol became serious. "I want you and Chrissy to go with me to Nashville. I don't want to go alone."

"But I'm not in love with Steve."

"Well, maybe not. That's your decision, but I still want you to make the trip with me."

"But, Carol, think about it. I don't want to mislead Steve or give him false hope."

"Maybe he's already aware of how you really feel toward him?"

Carol trusted Julie and understood her reason for not wanting to make the trip, but Carol had fallen for Jerry and wanted to join him. Still, she didn't want to lose Julie as a friend.

Julie became quite serious and spoke pensively.

"Carol, I didn't get a chance to tell you, but I've been promoted to assistant manager at the cafe. I'll be getting an increase in salary. I've managed to save a good chunk of money to start my antique business. I just can't leave all this, my dream would be shattered."

"Please, Julie, just try it. Who knows? Maybe you'll have a change of heart toward Steve. But even if not, we'd still be together. Think of the fun we could have!"

"Carol, you know I think the world of you and our friendship. Let me think it over."

Then she added, more reservedly, "Steve took me in his arms last night, and said he was in love with me and wanted Chrissy and me to join him. He said he would find a cozy place for us to live because he figured the band would be there for some time while trying to make a record album after the contest. I didn't say anything, but I have developed some sense of friendship toward him. It's just that it doesn't necessarily give me the desire to go with him. Then, as weird as it sounds, Brad flashes across my mind and I feel a pang of lonesomeness for him. I never said anything to Steve about Brad, but I think about Brad often. Course, I haven't heard from him except for that one letter shortly after he arrived in the Gulf."

"I understand your confusion, Julie, but Steve's a great guy. If you join him, you and I could still be together. And who knows what could happen after that?"

"Steve will be coming over tomorrow before the band's last performance so I'll sleep on the idea and let you all know then."

Saturday afternoon arrived. Jerry and Steve made a last visit before heading out for their last gig at the Blue Owl. The men, carrying another six pack of beer, greeted them with a rather ruckus show of enthusiasm. "Onward to the country music contest," as they good-naturedly slapped each other on the back. After some small talk, Steve asked Julie to join him in the kitchen.

"Julie, do you know how much it would mean to me if you'd join me in a couple of weeks? Once I get there I'll find a place for us which will be as comfortable as I can make it."

"But what about my home? I just can't leave it sitting here."

"You can close it up for now. You can phone back to a real estate agent and put it up for sale once we get settled."

Steve put his arms around Julie and told her again that he loved her. He attempted to kiss her on the mouth, but she turned her head.

Carol and Jerry remained in the living room sitting with their arms around one another and planning their reunion. It was a brief visit, and after sentimental farewells, the two men left for dinner and their last performance at the club.

Three days after Julie's last meeting with Steve, he phoned to tell her the band had arrived in Wisconsin for its final week of touring before heading to the contest. He had located a real estate firm which would find him a rental furnished condo while in Nashville. He also shared that he had spoken to the other musicians about her so that there would be no misunderstanding about the necessity for them to locate their own living quarters. Jerry was planning on Carol joining him and the three married fellows would be staying together in their own apartments. Jerry was also in the process of looking for a condo or apartment for Carol and him.

Julie admitted that she had never been to Nashville and that she and Carol had decided to drive separate cars, but stay together on the trip just as a safety precaution. Steve sensed the uncertainty in Julie's voice. Was she hesitant to make the trip itself, or was she uncertain yet that she could be a part of his life, he wondered. The distance from Milaca to Nashville was about 1,100 miles, about a 20-hour drive. He encouraged her by suggesting he thought it was a wise decision on the girls' part to make the trip together and not lose one another on the drive. He promised he would find a town midway, locate a motel, and would arrange for the girls to have adjoining rooms. He also promised to send her some money for the trip and motel expenses, and said that Jerry was planning to do the same for Carol.

Julie found herself reluctantly agreeing with everything that Steve said. Yet, there was a lingering feeling of loneliness she just couldn't explain or figure out. She had decided Steve was truly in love with her, and she was glad that she had made the decision to go to Nashville, though a bit surprised at herself for doing so. She would still be with Carol, which gave her a feeling of comfort about making the trip. Her employer had already given her a leave of absence. Still, she was skeptical about the appropriateness of her decision.

Julie's thoughts turned to the letter from Brad in which he expressed his sincere and devoted love for her, but now he was thousands of miles away and she may never see him again. Was that what was nagging at her? Did Steve mean more to her than she had realized? Is there such a thing as true love? What was it that was tugging at her heartstrings and kept pulling her thoughts back and forth? Her mind settled down following the wavering of choices that came involuntarily into her thinking about love, infatuation, Steve and Brad.

Her wanderings were interrupted when she was brought back to reality by Steve's question.

"Gee, you've been awfully quiet. Are you okay? Not having second thoughts, are you?"

"No, I'm fine. Just thinking about my house, actually. I'll lock it up and give the key to my neighbor, Ben. I'm sure he won't mind checking it for me until I decide if I want to sell or rent it."

Julie decided it might be difficult to have Ben involved in the equation if she wasn't going to be honest enough to tell him about her trip with Steve. Though he had always been gracious and never too forward about offering his opinions with regard to her personal life, she liked when he would make a suggestion or offer a bit of advice about the things going on in her life. She and Ben had had more than one discussion about the men in her life. Ben had some very specific opinions about it all, but his fatherly attitude toward her gave him the freedom to be frank and explicit about those with whom he did not think she should associate. Sometimes she took Ben's advice, but it seemed to Ben that most of the time she used him as a sounding board and would pursue her own thinking about her male preferences anyway.

Again Steve interrupted her daydreaming with a question. "Who is this Ben?"

"I've known him for a while now. We're neighbors and friends with one another. He's a retired lawyer from the Twin Cities. He used to come in the cafe where I worked each noon with his wife until her condition had deteriorated to a point where he could not handle her any more. If he heard I was doing something he thought might not be in my best interest, I'm sure he'd have some friendly words of caution for me. In many ways, he's become a father to me, I guess."

"Well, then, you'll have somebody you trust who can check your place until you sell it. You know I love you and want to take care of you and Chrissy forever."

"Thanks, Steve. I know you do. I'll wait to hear from you when you get to Nashville so Carol and I can get ready for the trip."

She hung up the phone and without any particular forethought walked into the bedroom and retrieved Brad's letter from the top drawer. She read it twice, aloud, as if reading it aloud would somehow clarify her own thoughts for her.

"Brad, I've been trying to sort out my feelings for you for a long time. I think of you from time to time, but were we actually meant for each other? Today, I guess I don't know. I've met this good man. He says he loves me. Maybe you and I will meet again. Maybe we won't. Right now, this feels like something I have to do. I can't explain it, not even to myself, but I have to do this."

Julie put the letter back in her dresser, walked to the phone, and dialed Ben's number.

"Julie, what a nice surprise. It's been a while since I've heard from you. How are you, my dear?"

"Yes, it has been a while, hasn't it? Actually, I'm calling to see if Chrissy and I can come over for a visit later today. Say about 3?"

"C'mon over. I'd like a visit."

As Ben opened the door, he was greeted by Julie and Chrissy, who ran up to him and threw her arms around his neck. It did the old man's heart good to have the affection of a small child, especially one who was so willing to allow him to play the surrogate grandpa. Ben would often see her playing in the yard, or swinging on the swing set, and think how lovely it would be to have such a bright, precocious child as part of his life, if only on a limited basis. He had grown quite fond of Chrissy, and she of him. It was, as far as he was concerned, a match made in heaven.

Ben offered Julie and Chrissy the chairs on each side of the stone fireplace, while he sat down in his usual place on the sofa.

"I couldn't help but notice that you and your friend had some visitors the last couple of days. Are they local boys?"

"No. We met them this past week. They're in a country band on their way to Nashville. They just did a week's tour at the Blue Owl."

Ben's paternal curiosity was obviously aroused.

"Traveling musicians, huh?" he asked trying not to sound too protective or invasive.

"I know what must be going through your mind, but they came down to our table during intermission and introduced themselves. Their names are Jerry Cramer and Steve Palmer. They're from a small town out west. The group has played together since they all were in the same high school. All the guys are in their mid-twenties, but Steve and Jerry are the only two who are single."

"Ahh," he said rather pensively. "I couldn't help but notice that the little car they had was at your place three days in a row."

Julie sometimes felt that Ben was a bit more inquisitive than a neighbor should be, especially when it pertained to her personal life. She knew Ben had taken a more than neighborly interest in her and Chrissy and that he was fond of both of them. Still, she felt quite comfortable most of the time in explaining her intimate affairs to him.

Ben was concerned that Julie not be enticed into an affair that could become a nightmare to her. He felt that there was a certain naivete in her responses to what others were telling her.

"Well, Ben, I'll tell you what has happened. When the guys came down between sets to talk to us, they asked us to stay after they were finished performing because they wanted to talk to us about visiting us the next day at my home. Carol and I agreed to the visit."

"So that was their car at your house."

"Uh, huh. Carol is crazy about Jerry and he's just as sold on her. Steve, the band leader, is really handsome and a great guy. When Steve came back to visit me the next day he admitted that he had fallen in love with me.

He's asked me to meet him in Nashville. They're competing in a contest there. He's really a nice person, Ben. I think you'd like him."

"Well, Julie, if he's a friend of yours, I don't doubt that he's a nice fella and that I'd like him. But how do you feel about him? Are you sure this is something you want to do?"

"I'm certain, at least at this precise moment, that I'm not in love with him, but he's the kind of guy who would be good to Chrissy and me, and I would be with Carol. But, truthfully, Brad keeps haunting my thoughts and I still have serious feelings for him."

Ben was beginning to feel uneasy about what she was telling him. He knew Julie was 25 years old, had a difficult first marriage and was in need of a man who would give her the companionship she now lacked. He didn't want to intrude in her life and tell her what his real concern was about the Nashville trip. However, Ben's did want to talk about Brad.

"I wonder how Brad is getting along in the Persian Gulf?" he mused aloud, hoping to ascertain what Julie's real feelings for Brad were.

"I've received only one letter from him. He phoned me before he left and told me he loves me. He also told me he loves me as much as ever in the letter. I think of him often but we haven't seen each other since last summer except once. He did phone me frequently through the fall and early winter. He was apparently wrapped up with his law profession and city friends."

Ben was aware that, for the most part, Julie tended to keep her feelings to herself, especially about her love affairs. However, he couldn't help but remember when she was with Brad at the Bar Association convention, the attention she gave to him, the fun they seemed to have together and her appearance of being in love with him.

"Well, if you're satisfied that you're doing the right thing and are happy about it, it's your decision. I sensed when you phoned me that you might want my opinion on the young man visiting you, but that's all I can say. I don't know him so obviously I can hardly venture an opinion beyond what I've already given you."

"Thanks, Ben. I think I'm doing the right thing for Chrissy and me, but it's going to be hard to leave here, to leave my home, relatives, and, of course, my neighbors. I won't be leaving for a couple of weeks. I'll stop and say good-bye before I go. I haven't put my house up for sale yet. Actually, I'm still not sure what I'll do about that, but it's a decision I can make later on depending on how things go with Steve."

With Chrissy in hand, Julie walked across the street and back to her own home. She was glad she had talked to her neighbor and knew what his opinion on her latest venture was. She felt better about her own decision to meet Steve in Nashville. Chrissy had not yet started school, so Julie felt relieved that she would not have to pull Chrissy away from anything important in her life in order for her to make the trip.

The days passed quickly. There were numerous phone calls from Steve along the way to Nashville, and then the eventful call arrived.

"We're in Nashville. I've found a furnished condo for rent in Inglewood, a suburb, not far from the Cumberland River. The condo is on the ground level, part of a group of four condos in one building. It has a master bedroom and bath, two other bedrooms, a living room, dining room, kitchen, family room, and main bathroom. There is a patio off the lower level with a deck built over it. How does that sound, Julie?"

"Sounds great. What color carpeting does it have?"

"Light green and your feet sink into it when you walk over it."

"Wonderful."

"I've made arrangements for you, and Jerry has for Carol, at a motel outside Springfield, Illinois, where you can stay on your way down. It's about halfway, and with an early start you should reach the motel by dinnertime. I'm sending you a map that has the highways marked to take you to Nashville. I've sent you enough money to cover the trip. You should get it tomorrow."

Julie phoned Carol who had just heard from Jerry. He encouraged her to seriously think about leaving early on the day after tomorrow. Both the women spent the day prior to the trip getting their cars serviced, their clothes in shape and their houses in order to leave. They made sure they had their maps of travel, the money that was sent to them and the location in Nashville where they would meet Steve and Jerry.

It was an adventure they both were looking forward to.

## Chapter 14

THE WAR WAS IN FULL SWING. Brad was navigating a C-130 Hercules airplane. He had sent Julie his address but had yet to receive a letter from her. He still felt the same way about her as he did when he saw her the past summer. The photos of her hanging over his cot only partially satisfied his longing for her and the desire to be with her again.

He knew Julie would probably date once in a while, and he often winced and even paniced at the thought that she could date someone who might capture her heart. Would she be vulnerable enough to fall in love, perhaps even commit herself to someone else while he was gone. Sometimes it was all too painful to really think about, especially in the environment he now found himself. The reality of war hit him shortly after his arrival in the heat and sand of the Arabian Desert. He felt confident that he was doing his part to try to accomplish by the Western Allies a quick and successful end to the war, but his thoughts of Julie, their time together on the law cruise and convention, and when they met at her home, were what kept him going. His trust in her did not fade, nor had his love for her weakened.

Brad performed his duties masterfully. He made a number of trips each day from his base in southern Saudi Arabia to King Khalid Military City, not far from the Iraqi border, transporting personnel and equipment in the hold of the huge aircraft.

As his plane flew back and forth on these transport duties, he became intrigued with the long trench built by the Iraqi army just inside the Iraqi border. It extended from the south end of Kuwait up to a half-way point on the Iraqi-Saudi Arabia border. The trench, five feet deep and twelve feet wide, was filled with oil. Beyond it were wood stakes one foot apart around which barbed wire had been woven.

There was constant activity by the American transportation units in moving army tanks and armored vehicles, along with medical evacuation corps and equipment to the border. Ammunition dumps were built all along the way to the border. Medical and hospital facilities were built at the base.

Brad was assigned tent quarters during the layover at King Khalid Military City. During the night, Brad would be awakened by the screaming motors of the F-15C Eagles and F-16D combat planes and bombers, as entire air wings would take off directly over his tent on their missions into Iraq.

While he lay on his cot, trying to sleep, arms folded under the back of his head, he wondered about Julie and what she was doing in his absence. He could still visualize her with her flowing dark hair as it fell against the background of her white blouse, purple slacks and white shoes.

How he wished he had been able to see her once more before he left for the Gulf. He wanted to tell her just how much he loved her and ask her to marry him. He still kept the trust he had in her and hoped the trust he felt was warranted. His intuition told him that she might become involved with another man, but he had to remove such thoughts from his mind if and when they arose. Sleep evaded him. He missed her. He needed her. He located some note paper and an envelope and addressed it to her home.

Dear Julie:
I think of you constantly. I miss not being able to phone you on weekends and being unable to drive to your home to visit you.

All of my memories are about the wonderful times we had together. The trauma of war is stressful, but I am comforted by my thoughts and dreams of us being together. You will never know how much I hope, we will be together again so that I can take care of you and Chrissy. I miss your eyes, your smile, and our good times together.

My engagements in battle are changing daily but I expect to get an address soon for your letters.

Love,

Brad

The M-551 Sheridan tanks, the M-60 tanks, and great M-1 Abrams tanks roared by his quarters as they moved into position near the border. M270 rocket launchers and numerous Humm-Vee with 12.7 millimeter machine gun on their roofs passed by his quarters on the way to the front. As the war escalated and the tanks moved into Iraq, they were accompanied by Black Hawk fighter planes and AH-64 Apaches. Precision radar was able to locate Iraqi equipment and personnel and to guide the tanks, planes, helicopters, and ground personnel on their strikes within Iraq.

Troops in two and one-half ton jeep trucks with about ten men to a carrier continued to move toward the front to flush out the enemy and solidify those areas that had been taken in the fighting.

As each night approached, the battle roared on. Brad could not settle down in his tent for a rest so pronounced was the pitch of battle, the sirens screaming their warning of multiple Scuds headed toward targets at Military City and other targets in Saudi Arabia. King Khalid Military City was a prime target for destruction by the Iraqis. The flame of the Scud motors, which showed them cruising about one and a half miles in the air headed for the city, were clearly visible to the eye. Eight-foot-deep underground bunkers were built with supports for coverings that would withstand any equipment driven over the bunkers during enemy air raids to give some protection to personnel from the enemy fire.

As the allied equipment moved toward the battle, the steel treads on the huge tanks rumbled and clanked when they moved around their axles, thrusting the tanks forward through the desert sands leaving their tracks behind. Army engineers, equipped with bulldozers, backhoes, scrapers and large graders, proceeded into enemy territory along with the huge army tanks breaking down barriers, filling oil trenches so that tanks could cross them, removing or destroying any other impediments to the allied armies' forward march. While watching the battle from the navigator's chair in his aircraft, Brad realized the danger he was encountering. He feared he might never see Julie again. He wondered what Julie and Chrissy would do with their lives if he was not part of them.

The air strikes into Iraq were constant throughout both the day and night, many of them emanating from the massive air bases near Military City. Landing and taking-off strips had been installed during Desert Shield so that the combat planes had sufficient runways from which to release a number of air wings into the sky to head for enemy targets in Iraq.

Brad's C-130 landed on the cement runway of Military City to refuel after one of its flights on which it carried personnel and equipment into areas close to the Iraqi-Saudi border. Desert Storm was two weeks old and at the height of the endeavor to defeat the enemy and drive it out of Kuwait. As the sun set and darkness overtook the sky, the sirens began to wail again, signaling the onslaught of Scuds. Some of them were obviously aimed at Military City.

The army had placed a number of Patriot Missile Batteries around both King Khalid City and Military City. The batteries consisted of clusters of four missiles in each battery and were built on moveable trucking equipment large and heavy enough to withstand the explosive delivery. As the Scud missiles began to show their fiery track against the dark background of the night sky, the Patriot Missile Batteries went into action rocketing into the sky to meet the incoming Scuds.

Brad, along with other personnel, left their tents to head for the nearest underground bunker. Brad felt duty bound to check on his aircraft parked on the side of the runway, about 300 yards from the bunker to which he was going. As he ducked around the evacuated tents and passed personnel headed for the various bunkers, there was a loud, bright explosion directly overhead as the Patriot missiles met their targets. The impact sprayed hot metallic debris through the air. Some of the debris crashed into the ground and runway just a short distance from where Brad was running to get to his assigned bunker.

Suddenly, he felt a sharp sting in his left thigh. He crumpled to the ground. When he finally stood up on his right leg and looked at the left leg of his uniform, he saw a tear in his uniform about a foot in length just above the knee. Blood was beginning to ooze from a wound caused by a piece of shrapnel lodged in his leg.

He realized he would have to crawl to the nearest bunker when he saw four soldiers leap from the bunker. They lifted him onto a stretcher and then crept back to the bunker. Their immediate response to Brad kept him from being further injured by more falling debris.

A siren in the distance signaled that an air base ambulance was on the way. Once on the scene, a medic began to attend to Brad. He cut off the left pants leg of Brad's uniform, removed left sock and shoe and applied a tourniquet to his upper thigh with a torn piece of bed sheeting. They sped off to the nearest medical unit complete with hospital facilities, doctors, nurses, and paramedics.

At the hospital compound Brad was carried into the operating room where doctors and nurses were waiting to attend to him. Once anesthetized, the doctors discovered that Brad had suffered a fracture of his left femur, as well as damage to the muscles supporting the femur. The doctors needed to realign the broken pieces of the bone after cutting through the skeletal muscle around the fracture. Because of the nature of the fracture, it was decided to form a union of the broken pieces of bone internally by inserting a plate with metal screws to hold the broken parts of the bone together.

The fracture was immobilized. The doctors agreed that Brad would eventually be able to walk on crutches, and later a cane until the fractured femur had completely unified.

In the recovery room Brad awakened to the sound of sweet, gentle voices and the constant talk of one smiling face bent over him.

"How are we doing? Feeling alright?"

"Uh, huh, but my left leg hurts like crazy."

The young nurse smiled. "I'm not surprised. That was quite an injury and you were under for quite a while."

"I still feel really fuzzy."

The nurse attending Brad informed him that an orderly would be in soon to help him into quarters in the hospital with three other men. She would be one of his nurses while he was recuperating. Brad managed a half-hearted smile and fell back asleep.

Brad's nurse was an attractive young woman of much the same build as Julie but with auburn hair and hazel eyes. After he was moved into his own hospital bed, he was placed on intravenous feeding together with a fluid of antibiotics to offset any infection. The same young nurse in the recovery room began checking on him, usually on an hourly basis. A short time after

Brad had been moved to his own bed, a staff doctor visited him.

"Well, young man. Quite an injury you sustained. We had to put a plate and screws in your left thigh to keep the broken bone in place so it will heal and make a better union. You'll need to stay off it for a few weeks, but you should be able to walk on it with the help of crutches. Not to worry. We'll have you up and around in no time. Meanwhile, the nurses will assist you. Don't want you taking a tumble and undoing all my handiwork," he said with a warm smile.

Brad settled back in his bed, thanked the doctor, and turned to watch for the young nurse to come back. She returned shortly after the doctor left.

"Is there anything you'd like, or can I help you in some way?"

"Yes, could you tell me who you are? Could you tell me your name? I noticed you speak with an accent, but I can't quite tell what it is."

She leaned over Brad so he could hear her whisper, "My name is Yvonne Fraser from Toulouse, France. I'm with a French unit working with the American nurses here."

"You speak good English. Your accent is barely noticeable."

"I studied English at the Berlitz Language School while I was also studying to become a nurse."

"Do you have a family?"

"Yes. My parents still live just outside Toulouse, but I haven't seen them for a number of months."

Brad was caught off guard by his attraction to this beautiful young woman. It surprised him that he couldn't wait for her to come back after she'd leave.

Brad stayed bed bound for almost a week. He was recuperating well and getting anxious to start moving about a bit. Yvonne's next visit was a pleasant one.

"Now you must get up and try to walk with a crutch. Come, I will help you. Swing around and I will put the crutch under your left arm. Then I will steady you as we go for a walk."

Brad stood up on his right leg and put the crutch under his left arm.

"Now, put your right arm around my shoulders to give you support while we walk."

Brad welcomed her assistance as he put his right arm about Yvonne's shoulders while she walked him about the hospital quarters. She would tell him from time to time to put a little weight on his left leg to strengthen it and to shift some of his body weight onto his left side. Brad followed Yvonne's instructions carefully and obediently. He wanted to be released from the infirmary as soon as possible and be able to get out from under its confines. Yet he was enjoying the attention he was receiving from Yvonne. He liked having her near him.

Had Brad found a new love or was Yvonne a lovely distraction from a lost love? She was very pretty. and she was very attentive to him. Perhaps she was fond of him as well.

Brad's activity in the war, and now his recovery from his injuries, had considerably contributed to the absence of letters to Julie. Yvonne managed to capture his attention almost fully. Still, there were times while recuperating that his thoughts returned to Julie. He still loved her, but doubts about her feelings for him often overwhelmed him.

After a week of physical therapy in the hospital, Brad was released with instructions to use his crutch for some time and then walk with a cane to support his left leg before he put his full weight on it. Yvonne walked into Brad's room the afternoon of his release and stood beside his bed.

"Good-bye, Brad. I've enjoyed working with you. I hope your leg heals quickly."

"Thanks, Yvonne. Can I see you once I'm discharged from the hospital?"

"Sure, Brad. You can reach me at the nurses' quarters. My phone number will be available at the hospital once I give them your name and let them know that you'll be phoning me."

Brad was pleased. He knew he wanted to see her again, to talk with her and go into King Khalid City together to one of the cafes. He had become very fond of Yvonne. He wanted to meet her again as soon as possible.

Brad was out of the hospital barely two days when he asked a friend in his tent quarters if he would drive him to the hospital. He wanted to get Yvonne's telephone number at the nurses quarters so he could phone her for a date. He phoned Yvonne during her off-duty hours.

"Would you join my friend and me tomorrow night on a trip into King Khalid City for dinner at the Royal Cafe?"

"I'd love to. Want me to set up a date for your friend?" she asked as they proceeded to finalize plans.

Yvonne was striking in her neatly fitting uniform which accentuated her curves. She was the kind of woman who commanded the attention of other patrons in the cafe. Brad was proud to be seen with her. Following a meal of curried chicken, whole potatoes, vegetables, and bottled water, the foursome returned to the military base. Brad asked Yvonne if she wanted to go for a walk before the skies darkened and the Scuds took to the air.

They walked along the edge of Military City, but within reach of the underground bunkers just in case the warning sirens of approaching Scuds filled the air. As they were strolling about, Brad showed her the C-130 Hercules airlift plane sitting on the runway.

"I'm assigned to an airlift group as a navigator. We move equipment and personnel in deployment to areas where the activity is hot. I was injured on a layover.

Odd that I would never have met you had I not been injured at this particular base, huh?"

"It does seem like quite a coincidence that we should meet under those circumstances."

"I've sure enjoyed being with you. Tell me about yourself."

Yvonne felt compelled to tell Brad about Michael, a medical officer in the French army, whom she had been seeing for a long time before she joined the French nurses auxiliary and volunteered to serve in Desert Storm.

"How about you, Brad? Where are you from and what did you do?"

"I'm from the Midwest part of the U.S., practicing law and serving in the Air Force Reserves."

"So you have a family, then, back in the States?"

"Yes, my folks are still alive, but I live alone."

"No girl friend?"

"Yes, and well, no, I guess. I thought I had found the girl I loved who lived in a small town in the northern part of my state. I'm relatively certain, however, that she doesn't love me. 'Course, I had to leave in such a hurry I didn't even get a chance to say good-bye hardly except for just a few minutes before I left and haven't heard from her since I've been here. But I am going to write her again and a friend of mine who's her neighbor."

Brad realized the evening was getting late and felt he should accompany Yvonne back to her quarters. He thanked her for the walk, which not only provided good exercise for his injured leg, but confirmed to him that he wanted to see more of Yvonne.

When he returned to his quarters, he decided to write to both Julie and Ben, tell them about his injury, and ask them to write back. He told Julie that he still loved her, that he hoped he would be home soon, and that he wanted to see her every free weekend when he returned to the states.

To Ben he wrote about the weather, sand conditions, and inquired as to how he was getting along. He also asked Ben to check on Julie and Chrissy and to write him back about them. As he sealed the envelope, he was startled to suddenly realize how much he regretted not having seen Julie during the fall before he left for the Gulf.

After writing the two letters, he laid back in his cot, put his hands under his head and reminisced about the good times he and Julie had had together. He had become quite fond of Yvonne, but there was still that heart and soul feeling for Julie and the hope that some day maybe she would love him.

Brad phoned Yvonne again the next time his aircraft group was at Military City on an airlift mission. He had now discarded his crutches, but continued to use a cane to take the weight off his left leg. He picked up Yvonne at the base hospital. She was again clad in her nurse uniform with her auburn hair tucked up under her French nurse's hat. They walked along the runway and various quarters of Military City.

"The war seems to be favoring the Allies and, hopefully, the end is in sight. What do you plan to do after the war is over?"

"I expect to return to France and probably return to the hospital where I worked before the war. Then there's also Michael. He's been writing to me regularly and has asked me to marry him."

Brad was a bit surprised. Yvonne had only casually mentioned Michael during their previous visits. Still he said he was happy for her. As she talked, Brad understood that she was in love with her doctor who was interning at the hospital where she had worked and that he was, in fact, just a nice diversion from the war and work. Unexpectedly, he felt a sense of relief that she was committed, though it caught him off guard, as well.

"How about you, Brad? What are you going to do after this is over?"

Brad said that his law firm would take him back and he would remain in the Air Force Reserves.

"But, Brad, what about the young lady with whom you are in love? Aren't you going to try to see her again?"

"I wrote her recently and informed her that I still

love her as much as ever and that I wanted to see her more often, but I haven't heard back from her."

Brad said goodnight to Yvonne and wished her happiness in her future endeavors, professionally and personally. He returned to his quarters to find a letter from Ben.

Dear Brad,

I certainly was surprised to receive a letter from you. It's unfortunate that you suffered the injury to your leg, but, I'm glad to hear you have had excellent medical attention and are making a good recovery.

I'm writing you about Julie and Chrissy with some reluctance because I'm still uncertain as to what took place. Julie came over to talk to me about two members of a country western band whom she and her girlfriend, Carol, met at the Blue Owl Inn while the band was on a tour stop on their way to Nashville.

Although I have not met Steve, I did see him and his buddy at Julie's house for a couple hours on three consecutive days. Julie talked about Steve and said she and Carol were going to meet the two men in Nashville. She closed up her house, but I do not think she put it up for sale.

I can't tell you much more about Julie or Chrissy because I haven't heard from her since she phoned to tell me she had arrived in Nashville.

Sincerely,

Ben

Extremely disheartened after reading the letter, Brad put his head down in his hands and sighed aloud.

"My Julie's gone. I should have gone up to see her more before I left for this blasted war. How could she do such a thing? She knew I loved her, but obviously she didn't love me. I don't think I can love anyone but her."

Brad shoved the letter in his pocket, picked up his cane, and ambled over to the officers' off-duty quarters. He saddled up to the bar to drown his sorrows and soon began laughing and joking with the other officers at the bar. But the laughter was hollow and the jokes were a ruse. Inside he was heartbroken.

*Chapter 15*

It didn't take Julie or Carol long to find the building in which Steve and Jerry had rented condos. The neighborhood was on the outskirts of Nashville near high-rises, schools, and playgrounds. In one of the telephone conversations Julie had with Steve before she left Milaca, he told her that an extra set of keys would be available to her at the building office in the event the band was tied up at the time of the women's arrival. Julie picked up the keys to the condo registered to Stephen Palmer, and with Chrissy and her luggage, proceeded to head for her new home. Carol, too, picked up her keys and went to Jerry's place.

Julie was immediately impressed with the layout of the two floors of furnished rooms. A quick walk through the unit disclosed a combination living room and dining room, kitchen, two bedrooms, fireplace, bathrooms, laundry room. A balcony with wrought iron railing was built off the dining room. As Julie walked back near the entrance way, she noticed a note on the table by the door.

"Hope you enjoy the place. Find beer, pop and wine in the refrigerator. You, Carol and Chrissy relax. Jerry and I should be back about 5 p.m. after rehearsal. Love, Steve."

The drive had been tiring and both Julie and Carol were grateful to be able to plot into a cozy chair and sip a glass of wine. Chrissy found some children's entertainment on TV and happily settled down for a while.

"This is the life, isn't it, Julie?"

"Certainly is different from what I'm accustomed to. It almost seems like a dream."

Carol had been to her own condo before showing up at Julie's. Carol obviously relished the change in her lifestyle as she stood in the center of the living room and whirled about holding the glass of wine without spilling a drop. Julie seemed more collected about it all and smiled wryly as she looked about the rooms and furnishings. Neither of the girls had been exposed to this way of life. Was this what they really wanted?

The door opened and in walked Steve and Jerry with cartons of chow mien for dinner. As they closed the door Jerry joked.

"I knew Carol would be with Julie, so we both headed for Steve's layout."

Carol beamed in Jerry's direction.

"I looked at ours, and it's wonderful. Then I joined Julie to rest a while after the long drive."

"Did everything go okay on the trip? Did you have enough money to cover expenses?" questioned Steve.

"Yes, we stayed together on the highway, ate together, and our motel rooms were next to each other. Everything went off without a hitch."

"Good. Let's have a drink to celebrate."

The women held up their wine glasses and the men their cans of beer. Jerry gave a toast to their arrival.

They ate while the food was hot and sat quietly for a while, letting both their food and their thoughts have time to digest.

Carol and Jerry left. Julie turned to Steve.

"How's the planning and rehearsals coming for the contest?"

"Gosh, there are a lot of bands competing so we've been rehearsing some really long hours each day."

"What do you think your chances are of winning?"

"Well, right now we're feeling pretty confident. We're hoping to make a record at one of the studios in town, if we get the chance, and get some money from that to help finance us. We have some left from earnings on the way."

Julie sensed the struggle Steve must be going through to keep his band going while trying to make it a contest winner and possibly a celebrity band. Steve had saved some money from earlier performances, but he realized the band needed publicity to provide a steady income for them all.

Julie respected Steve for his courage in getting the band as far as he had in the music industry. She knew, too, that in addition to a top performance, it would need a break in the business to reach the kind of popularity which would give them notoriety in the industry.

Her thoughts shifted. She suddenly realized how uncertain she really felt about Steve. One thing was certain. She did not love him. Should she keep her distance while still comforting and helping him? She wasn't quite sure what he expected of her.

Several hours later Carol and Jerry returned. Julie prepared dinner for all of them. Following the meal and putting the dishes in the dishwasher, they decided to watch a little TV before retiring. About 10:30 p.m. Julie suggested that they turn in, admitting she was tired from the trip. Jerry and Carol made their way to the door.

"Good night, you two. We'll see you in the morning."

Awkwardness filled the room. Steve, Julie, and Chrissy were alone together. Steve walked up to Julie and put his arms around her waist.

"Julie, I missed you. I'm so glad to see you and Chrissy." She did not attempt to push him away.

"I'm glad the trip is over and we can settle down for a while."

"Want another beer?"

"No, thanks. I'm tired, and I think Chrissy and I should get some sleep."

"Have you seen the master bedroom?"

"Uh, huh. I made a tour of the place just after we arrived. The bedroom is beautiful."

"And Chrissy can sleep in the second bedroom down the hall and use the main bathroom."

Julie removed herself from Steve's arms slowly but deliberately.

"I'll sleep with Chrissy tonight. She'll be out of her own room and bed and might be scared the first night in a strange place."

Steve looked chagrined. "Okay, but if you need anything, let me know."

Had he misjudged Julie's reactions and feelings, he wondered. Why had she made the long trip if she didn't want to be with him? Had she been so wounded from her past marital experiences? Steve felt he loved Julie very much, but he was disturbed by this rebuff on their first night together under a plan which he had devised for their future together.

Julie took Chrissy by the hand and headed for the second bedroom with her luggage.

"Good night, Steve. See you in the morning."

When they were alone in their own bedroom, Julie told Chrissy, "Tomorrow we'll write to Ben and let him know we got here all right. We'll give him the address and phone number here, too."

Chrissy crawled into the large queen size bed and cuddled up on big soft pillows with Julie lying next to her. Julie's mind raced. Down the hall there was a man who told her he is in love with her. But a feeling of nostalgia or longing for something or somebody prevented her from falling asleep. Could it be Brad who haunted her mind? She shrugged off such thoughts by trying to justify that being with Steve at this time was the best solution for her and Chrissy. But something kept nagging at her that would not leave her at complete rest.

A bright and sunny morning peeked through the yellow shutters covering the bedroom windows. As she folded back the shutters, Julie looked out at numerous high-rises that stood straight in the air along a street which appeared to be at the bottom of a canyon. She and Chrissy had slept until midmorning. Quietness pervaded the rest of the condo.

She showered, and then bathed Chrissy. Steve was not to be found and had apparently left without awakening them. While she was making some coffee for herself and breakfast for Chrissy, the front door bell rang. Julie opened the door to be greeted by Carol.

"Good morning. May I come in? We had breakfast already, but I'll have a cup of coffee with you," as she headed toward the kitchen with Julie.

Carol, obviously in a positively cheery mood, continued on.

"Hope you slept all right last night."

"Yes, Chrissy and I must have been exhausted because

we slept until the middle of the morning. We've only been up for about a half hour."

"You and Chrissy slept together? I thought you and Steve were in love."

"You know I like him, and I may even be interested in him, but that doesn't mean I have to sleep with him the first night I'm here. Besides, I was concerned that Chrissy and I both got a good night's sleep on our first night away from home."

Carol was exuberant as she threw her shapely legs over the stuffed arm rest of the lounge chair.

"Jerry and I made love last night. He proposed to me and thinks we should get married soon. I'm really in love with him, Julie. It felt so right to be in his arms last night."

Julie let out a little gasp, hesitated for a minute or two to say anything, then answered.

"I've had a sick feeling ever since I've been here that I'm not doing the right thing. You and I are good friends so I know I can level with you. I dreamed about Milaca last night."

"Does Steve know how you feel?"

"I don't know, but he appeared dismayed when I said I was sleeping with Chrissy after he explained about the master bedroom which he and I would be sharing."

Carol felt it best to say nothing and suggested a walk to the nearest playground and a visit to a nearby park.

Their high-rise was built on a street not far from a both a park and an elementary school.

The three of them acted as if they were in a new world. This certainly was different from Milaca.

At lunchtime they found a fast food restaurant which had a playground on its premises.

"You know, Carol, I think I like this way of living. This city is beautiful."

"Well, I know I like it, and I'll be with Jerry. He's a good man who loves me and I love him. How much better does it get than that?"

When Julie, Carol, and Chrissy arrived back at the condo, Jerry and Steve were already at the kitchen table with a calculator going over papers full of figures.

Both men stood up to embrace the girls as they walked into the kitchen. Julie stood still and turned her head when Steve tried to kiss her on the lips.

Steve was not deterred. "Julie, you look beautiful."

"Thanks. I feel better today. It was probably the long trip that tired me out."

The men resumed their paperwork so the women went into the living room to talk. Steve and Jerry emerged from the kitchen an hour later with looks of bewilderment on their faces. Carol immediately questioned them.

"You look worried. Is something wrong?"

"The music business is very risky and highly competitive. We haven't had any performances, just rehearsals, since we've been here. Frankly, things are getting a little tight, but I think we should be okay."

Jerry joined Steve. "We've been rehearsing like crazy to get ready for the contest, and looking for a studio that'll help us cut an album. The contest is coming up this weekend at the Grand State Opera House. We have tickets for you two and Chrissy."

"I have some money left from the trip. Let's all go out to a restaurant and eat," Julie said, trying to lighten the conversation.

The response of the group was unanimous. A small family cafe within walking distance of their condos offered great food, plenty of it, and all at a reasonable price. Despite the monetary concerns, the foursome enjoyed their evening out with light conversation and good-natured teasing among them.

The girls knew Steve and Jerry were struggling with finances so they suggested they go back to one or the other's condo and just watch TV for the evening. About 10:30 p.m. Carol said she was getting tired and that they should leave for their own place. Jerry agreed and quickly headed for the door to open it for Carol.

Now Julie was left alone with Chrissy and Steve. Almost immediately she again had that feeling of loneliness but she quickly rebounded back to Steve, who was now standing in front of her with his hands on her shoulders.

"Hey, Julie. Where were you? You looked as if you

were a million miles away for a minute there. Something on your mind that I can help you with?"

"It's nothing, Steve. But I should get Chrissy to bed."

Julie led Chrissy by the hand to their bedroom. After tucking her in, Julie returned in her red terry cloth pajamas and robe. Steve was sitting on the sofa reading the newspaper. As Julie sat down beside him, he dropped the newspaper and put his arm around her shoulder. She felt a certain comfort in Steve's strong arm, broad chest, and shoulders, as they sat for a few minutes with their eyes closed.

After a few minutes Julie looked at Steve and smiled. It had been a long time since Julie had felt the security of being held close by a man who told her he loved her very much. But was she in the arms of the man she loved? If she was not, could she learn to love Steve? He was a good man who had not forced her into questionable situations, and he was good to Chrissy, too.

Slowly, Julie began.

"You know, Steve, I've been wondering if I'm doing the right thing. Something tells me that I shouldn't have left home to come here. It's not because of you. I enjoy being with you. It's just I have this feeling. I can't explain it—it's just a feeling, ya know?"

"Julie, are you trying to tell me that you don't love me? If so, I can understand that. I mean, it's early in the relationship and some people need more time than others to know what they're feeling. But it makes no difference for now because I know I love you. And that's good enough for me, right now. I hope, in time, you'll love me, but the word here is "time," Julie. We have plenty of time."

Julie lifted her face to Steve's and he kissed her cheek in a tender, loving manner. They held the kiss for a long time, until Julie moved away saying, "Steve, I've got to sleep with Chrissy again tonight until I find myself."

Steve walked Julie to Chrissy's bedroom, slowly opened the door and quietly whispered, "Good night, Julie. I love you."

Steve instinctively knew not to push Julie sexually. His love for her went well beyond anything sexual. He wanted to be with her, to give her the attention she deserved, and to enjoy her beauty. As the days moved on, their lives fell into the same repetitious pattern until the night of the contest.

*Chapter 16*

THE GULF WAR WAS ENDING, but Brad was unable to get back on active duty roster because of his injury and the need to still use the cane to hobble about. The news of the war's end was somewhat unexpected at the time of its announcement, but an obviously huge relief to those men and women participating in it. In a few weeks, many of them would receive orders to return stateside to their home bases.

Ben's letter to Brad containing news of Julie's latest activities was disheartening to Brad, but his love for Julie was unshakable. Perhaps Ben was mistaken in his appraisal of Julie's latest relationship. Still, when his thoughts focused on her trip to Nashville with the country western musician, he knew something must have gone awry in his relationship with Julie.

With so much time on his hands, Brad mentally sorted through all the women he had known. Julie always came to the forefront as the woman he wanted for a lifetime. The image of her in her yard, the good times on the cruise, and her forthrightness about sexual matters always flashed into his mind to deter his suspicions about her new relationship. His thoughts about loving Julie weighed heavily upon his mind most of his awakened hours.

About two weeks after the war's end, Brad received a note to report to the chief navigator of his airlift group for further orders. He was going to be sent back to his home base in the states and be released to inactive duty. To report to the chief navigator who now was located at a base other than Military City where Brad was recuperating, he had to take the next airlift plane. When he reported to the chief navigator's office, he was handed his traveling orders with the explanation:

> "On the date shown on your orders you will be transferred by air to a debarking airlift in the United States for further transfer to your home base in your home state."

Brad smiled. He was going home! The administrative officer informed Brad he would be quartered at his present base while awaiting departure for the states and that it might be a week or two before the orders could be activated. As Brad retired to his quarters to await further action, he wrote to his family and the Larimores. He decided to drop a quick note to Ben.

Dear Ben,
    Today I received orders from my command that I'll be transferred by air to a base in the United States and

then to my home base within a week or two. I've been recuperating from the injury, but I'm now quartered at the base of my departure. I have ditched the crutch, but still use a cane for support. My leg does seem to be healing okay.

I have not heard from Julie. I think of her constantly, and I'm unable to get those thoughts out of my mind. Despite her new relationship, I still love her. I blame myself for not having visited with her more often last summer. I must confide to you that she is the only woman I love or ever will love.

I'm told my home base will have information of the time and date of our arrival at the base following our departure from Saudi. If I get any information in advance, I'll write you again.

Sincerely,

Brad

Ben received the letter within a week and immediately sat down at his desk and replied.

Dear Brad,
I was glad to hear from you and to learn that your recovery is going well and that you are headed home. Be assured I will contact your home Air Force base by phone to find out the projected date of your arrival. I plan to meet you when you arrive there.

I received a letter from Julie after she arrived in Nashville, but have not heard from her since. However, there is no 'For Sale' sign on her house, so I don't know what her current activities may be or what her plans are for the future.

Hope to see you soon.

>Sincerely,

>Ben

## Chapter 17

JULIE SPENT MOST of the late afternoon of the day of the contest getting ready to attend the show with Carol. She dressed in a low-necked long white dress with a high-heeled pump. She French-twisted her hair to add some maturity to her appearance. Chrissy wore her blue dress.

Carol's attire for the evening mirrored Julie's which made them both very striking and beautiful. Steve and Jerry had purchased tickets at such an early date that they were able to seat the women and Chrissy within ten rows of the stage.

Preliminary contests had been held during the week. Steve and Jerry's band was still in the running. The final contest was narrowed to the eight winners of the preliminary events. The programs given to the audience listed the results of the preliminary contests and the order of appearance of each of the bands. Steve and Jerry's was listed on the program as the eighth and final band to appear. Julie and Carol were both excited and nervous about which band would win. As the name Jayhawks was placed on stage, the women held hands.

As Steve, Jerry and the other band members came on stage, Steve and Jerry looked down at their two friends in the audience, smiled and winked. Julie caught Steve's eye as she raised her hand to give him a "V" for victory signal with her fingers. At the finish Julie, Carol and Chrissy clapped with all their might and enthusiasm. They weren't the only ones. The entire audience seemed overwhelmed by the excellence of the band and the judges voted unanimously for Steve and Jerry's band as the winners.

Once the contest was over, they all went to a celebrity cafe nearby to celebrate the victory and have dinner. About 1:30 a.m., everyone began to head home with greetings to one another on the success of the band.

Julie and Steve returned to their condo, but Steve left immediately to visit with his band members one-on-one to congratulate each of them more appropriately and specifically. He returned to find Julie curled up in her pajamas on the big sofa, sound asleep. He checked on Chrissy who was already sound asleep in her room. Steve returned to the living room and quietly walked over to Julie and kissed her on the forehead, waking her. She yawned and stretched away some of the grogginess.

"You and the band were excellent tonight. I'm really proud of you and everything you've accomplished."

Steve sat down beside her on the sofa and put his arm around her.

"This is a big break for us, Julie. I'm sure we'll be able to get a recording studio to help us make a record. There will probably be opportunities to go on tour, see the country, and maybe even the world. We'll have a great amount of promoting to do from now on. Think of the good times we'll have together."

"Steve, I'm happy for you, really I am, and Jerry and the others. You undoubtedly will have a great future to look forward to."

Steve tightened his embrace of Julie and expected her to respond, but after the conversation, she yawned again.

"It's been a big night and I'm really tired. I hope you don't mind if I turn in with Chrissy."

Steve was appalled and more than a bit shocked at Julie's attitude, but he refrained from expressing it.

"Okay, Julie. Sleep well. I'll see you in the morning."

He kissed her goodnight, and she joined Chrissy.

Again, Steve left early and Julie awoke to an empty house. The phone ringing broke the silence. It was Steve. He had just been offered a week's engagement at a large resort in a nearby state, a popular country western meeting place. The engagement provided quarters for only the band and he called to ask her what she thought of the deal.

"It's a great opportunity for you to promote the

band. I think you should go ahead Carol and I will be fine while you're away."

As the band members packed instruments and luggage into a large touring bus, there was lots of hugging and kissing to send the band off for their first major engagement. They hopefully were on their way to a successful career as a country western music band.

The Jayhawk's engagement at the resort lasted a week. On the day before the band was scheduled to return, Julie and Chrissy went to visit Carol.

Carol greeted them at the door and Chrissy scampered off to play. Julie looked more serious than usual.

"I have something I want to talk about with you."

They sat opposite each other on the big sofa. Carol chatted about the band and remarked how well Jerry and Steve were doing.

Julie agreed. "I'm really happy for them, but something keeps nagging at me. I'm so uncomfortable with all this. I keep thinking about my house and friends and folks back home. Sometimes Brad flashes across my mind, and I'm haunted by memories of my days with him."

"I understand, but you have a new life ahead of you with Steve. He's good to you and I'm sure he loves you. You can't give all this up now."

"But I'm not sure I'm doing the right thing by staying here. It's all really disturbing to me, Carol. Maybe

I'll feel differently tomorrow when Steve and the band return."

The band returned the following afternoon. Steve virtually flew through the door.

"Julie, dear, I'm back."

Julie walked up to Steve rather coolly, turned her cheek to receive his kiss and said, "Welcome home, Steve. I'm glad you're back safe and sound."

"Tonight we're going out to dinner to celebrate. We've had calls for bookings in some of the top resorts. Julie, it looks like we may be on our way."

Steve couldn't help but notice Julie's sobering countenance. It was obvious that something was troubling her. He took her by the hand and led her to the sofa.

"Julie, what's wrong? Did something happen while I was gone?"

Julie's hands flew up over her eyes as she began to sob. She was not usually an overly emotional person, but she could not control herself now. Her current state of mind and her relationship with Steve were weighing heavily upon her. Steve gently wiped her tears from her face.

"Steve, I've got to go back to my home. I haven't been able to sleep nights thinking about this."

As she talked, Brad vividly and clearly flashed across her mind, but she said nothing to Steve about this.

"Hon, aren't you happy here?"

"Sometimes. But there's a small voice that keeps telling me to go back. I can't explain the longing I have, although it's with me almost all the time."

"I love you, Julie, but if you're that unhappy here and need to go home, maybe you should. Let's still go out to dinner together tonight. Let me have just one more night with you, Julie, and tomorrow I'll help you get ready to go."

Julie felt a great sense of relief flood over her soul in that moment. Intuitively she knew she was doing the right thing for her and Chrissy. She couldn't wait to tell Carol about her decision. She knew, too, that Carol would stay with Jerry and not be returning to Milaca. Carol was right to stay. She was glad for her. And now, she was glad for herself.

That evening the foursome went to dinner together for the last time. They toasted the band's success and Julie's safe return to Milaca. The decision between Julie and Steve to part company was barely discernable from their exuberance at dinner. Julie packed her luggage early the next morning and, armed with a road map, she and Chrissy left for Milaca.

It was an uneventful trip home. Julie pulled into her driveway to find the snow piled high in the yard and around the house. She plodded through deep snow, opened the door and knelt down while grabbing Chrissy.

"Chrissy, honey, we're home at last."

As Chrissy ran to her own room, Julie trudged to the

car to get the luggage. Back in the house, she looked around at all the familiar surroundings and released a deep sigh of relief. She had no regrets about leaving Steve or Nashville. Brad's image, his voice, his proclamations of love for her now predominated all her thoughts. She couldn't get him off her mind.

Julie walked to the phone and just stood by it for a long time. She wanted to phone her neighbor, Ben, but after lifting the receiver she placed it back on the hook and walked away. She was overwhelmed with gratitude, and a bit of shame for having taken for granted all that she had here, her home, her family, even that her mother had thought to re-connect her phone before she arrived back. Yes, life was good here, with one exception. What about Brad? Where was he? How had he managed during the war? She went back to the phone. After a couple of tries at dialing and hanging up, she pulled herself together and got Ben on the line.

"Ben, I'm back from Nashville. May Chrissy and I come over to visit you tomorrow?"

"Welcome back! Sure, I'd love to talk to you. Oh, and by the way, I have some information about Brad."

Julie couldn't help but be excited. She could hardly wait until morning to find out about Brad. She barely slept that night and rose bright and early the next morning. There was laundry to do, the house needed some cleaning, there was snow to shovel off the sidewalk around the house and the driveway, but she completed it all before mid-morning. About 10:30 a.m. Julie phoned Ben.

"Chrissy and I are free for a visit if you are. Is this a good time?"

Ben welcomed Julie and Chrissy in and offered them a seat and cups of cocoa. Once everyone was settled comfortably, Ben began to ask about her trip to Nashville. Julie detailed the success of the band and its promising future. But what she most wanted was to ask him a question.

" Have you heard from Brad?"

"Yes, as a matter of fact I have. Let me share the latest news on him. You knew Brad was injured during the war and that the war is now over, didn't you?"

Julie sighed with apprehension. "What happened?"

"Well, according to his last letter, he'll be coming home soon. I don't know the exact date of his arrival, but I do know his leg took some shrapnel, but it's on the mend. I assume he'll arrive at his base within the next week or so, but I phoned his Reserve Base just yesterday to try to get the actual time and date of his arrival. So far, it's still not entirely clear when he'll get in."

Julie folded her hands nervously, moved forward in her chair and looked Ben straight in the eyes.

"Ben, I'm in love with Brad. I feel so foolish that I didn't recognize my feelings for him until I was already in Nashville. Shortly after my arrival there, I began to miss him desperately and I realized how much I loved him all along. I couldn't let another man touch me because of my sense of faithfulness to Brad. Steve is a fine person, but I'm not in love with him."

"Then you're sure you're in love with Brad? I know he loves you."

"There's no doubt in my mind now. But, will I ever see him again?"

"I plan to drive down to the base to meet him when he returns from Saudi Arabia. Would you like to join me?"

Julie's face broke into huge grin.

"Oh, could I? Yes, yes, I'd love to."

Ben promised to keep trying to get information about Brad's arrival date and to let her know a day or so ahead of the time as to when they'd leave. He asked Julie if she would help him drive part of the way. How pleased Julie was that everything was working out so beautifully. She was beside herself with anticipation of seeing Brad again. The days crawled by for Julie as she awaited Brad's return.

A week later the phone rang. It was Ben, and he had good news.

"Julie, Brad is due to arrive tomorrow at about 3 p.m. Let's drive down in the morning, have lunch together and then head for the air base."

"Chrissy and I will be ready at 8 a.m. Will that give us enough time?"

"That'll be perfect, dear."

Ben picked up the girls at about 7:45 a.m. He couldn't believe it, but he was actually as excited about the whole day as they were, and had to apologize for arriving before 8. The day was bright and mild. Julie was all smiles. They hopped in the car for what Julie believed would be one of the adventures of her life.

"I can't wait to see Brad again. I really do love him. I just hope he still loves me. I was so uncertain for a while, and that must have hurt him badly, but now I know he's the only one for me. You really know, don't you, Ben, when you truly love a person?"

"When I fell in love with my wife, I knew it was a true love. Love's not just a sexual attraction, but a compelling inner drive to want to be with someone forever, no matter what the prevailing conditions may turn out to be. You can always have a fondness or sense of compassion for others, but the feeling for the one you really love is an obsession and physical desire that consumes your entire life."

Julie appreciated Ben's explanation of love. She could relate to such an explanation by the way she felt about Brad. She was eager to see him and again be in his embrace. She wondered why she even had any doubt about her love for him during the past months. She had finally found herself and knew the doubts she had had were just imagined. She now had that deep down feeling that she belonged with him, and nothing was going to stop her from professing her love to him.

They stopped for lunch, the noon hour had passed, and it would be less than an hour before the plane carrying Brad was to land.

As Ben, Julie and Chrissy arrived at the Air Base, they observed a number of people already standing on the landing strip with American flags in their hands, their eyes scanning the sky. The February day was a crisp 20 degrees, but the bystanders were prepared for the chill and the blustering winds blowing across the runway.

Members of a Reserve Air Force Band huddled together with their instruments near the terminal. Their sparkling, bright uniforms brought an air of festivity to the scene.

A minute speck in the sky appeared in the distance, alerting the waiting crowd of a plane about to descent bearing the Persian Gulf returnees. The band moved from its huddle into a marching formation. A roar went up from the crowd as the plane came fully in sight and the band began its welcoming music. Julie grasped Ben's arm and held Chrissy's hand tightly as they stood together watching the wheels touch the runway. The plane taxied near the terminal where the returnees were to debark as the band filled the air with the strains of "The Saints Go Marching In."

Julie pulled her arm from Ben's as men and women

began to step out of the huge aircraft. Julie asked Ben to hang onto Chrissy's hand while she ran out to meet Brad. Suddenly, she saw him in the doorway of the plane. He moved out onto the landing with his cane. How handsome he looked wearing his deep blue airman's uniform and jacket over his shoulders. Tears filled her eyes as she realized the pain he must have suffered.

Brad descended the steps one at a time with the support of his cane and was about to step onto the runway when Julie ran toward him crying.

"Brad, Brad. You're back. You're really back!"

He immediately opened his arms to embrace her. He dropped his cane, and pulled her close to him as they stood together at the bottom of the steps embracing one another. She reached up to kiss him.

"Brad, I love you and always will."

"My Julie, my sweet, sweet Julie. I can't believe you're here."

Julie pointed to Ben standing at the side of the landing ramp holding Chrissy's hand. Brad grabbed Julie's hand and his cane and walked toward Ben and Chrissy. Ben was waiting with his hand extended.

"Welcome home, Brad."

Brad's family and the Larimores were also there to welcome him home. After greetings, he informed them that he'd see them in a day or two. Right now what he most wanted was to go home with Julie.

They walked through the terminal building to where Ben had parked.

"Brad, can you come to Milaca for awhile?"

"Yes, my dear, I want to."

Ben quickly joined the conversation.

"You can sleep at my place. I have a second bedroom."

"And it's just across the street," chimed in Julie.

Ben suggested to Chrissy that she ride up front so Julie and Brad could sit together in the back. Julie put her hand in Brad's.

"You don't know how good it feels to be with you again."

"And you, my dear, don't know how long I've waited for this moment," as he put his arm around her and pulled her closely to himself and whispered, "I love you."

Ben pulled up in front of Julie's house. Brad left his luggage in Ben's car as they all went in.

"I'll get some dinner started."

"That's too much work. Why don't we celebrate by going to the Pinewood Cafe!"

They all agreed on Brad's suggestion but decided to visit awhile before going.

Brad and Julie were cuddled next to each other on the sofa their eyes locked in an adoring gaze.

"Julie, will you marry me?"

"Oh, Brad. Yes, of course I will."

Brad retrieved a small case from his pocket.

"I still have the ring."

"Oh, Brad, it's so beautiful."

Ben and Chrissy walked over and stood in front of the sofa to witness the drama which was unfolding. Brad took her left hand in his and held the diamond ring in front of her wedding finger.

"Julie, I love you and I give you this ring to keep you forever."

He tenderly slipped the ring on her finger. Julie turned her face to his and they kissed unashamedly.

"Brad, I do love you with all my heart."

Chrissy was quite captivated by the whole event.

"It's so pretty, mommy."

Ben stood back a bit as a tear ran down his cheek.

"Congratulations. I'm so happy for you both."

Chrissy's plea for supper broke the atmosphere. They all just laughed and then left for the Pinewood Cafe. As they entered, all the waitresses turned and gazed at the foursome walking toward a booth. Suddenly one of the waitresses recognized Julie and hurried over to the foursome.

"I'd like you to meet Brad Owens. He's just returned from the war."

The waitress caught a glimpse of the diamond ring on Julie's finger and turned to one of the nearest waitresses.

"Julie's got a ring!"

Many of the patrons had known Julie for some time. Some applauded. Other waitresses made their way over to the booth to see Julie and to check out her ring. She introduced Brad to them who, at any time, would have been an immediate attraction in his war uniform.

"I'd like you all to meet my fiancée, Brad."

After dinner the foursome went back to Julie's, but Ben and Brad didn't stay too long. It had been a very full day for everyone and Brad admitted he was feeling tired.

Brad told Julie he'd go back to Minneapolis the next day to visit his relatives and the law firm. He phoned John Larimore who had volunteered to drive up to Milaca to get him.

"Julie, what do you say we get married this coming summer?"

"That would be wonderful."

"I'll come up this weekend. Can we plan our wedding then?"

"I can't wait, Brad."

The men walked back to Ben's for the night. The next morning John arrived to take Brad back to Minneapolis. Brad was at Julie's.

"Good-bye, my dear Julie. I'll be back in a few days. I love you."

Julie watched them drive away and then asked Chrissy to sit next to her on the sofa.

"Honey, Brad and I are going to get married. Do you understand that, Chrissy?"

"Sure, mom , it means we can all live together."

"You know, Chrissy, he's a wonderful man and I want to live with him the rest of my life." Chrissy clapped her hands.

"Me, too!"

"Chrissy, we'll have to leave here and live near Brad's work," explained Julie.

"It's okay, mom. We'll be fine, right?"

"Of course we will, honey."

Brad and John went directly to see Brad's folks and his younger brother. Brad could hardly contain himself.

"I have a surprise for all of you. Julie and I are engaged."

"Oh, Brad. We're so happy for you both."

Brad asked his folks if he could have his old room back until he and Julie had determined where they would live. The following day, dressed in a business suit, Brad went to his law firm. His old office had since been occupied, but other space was provided for a new office and new equipment. He met John for lunch in the restaurant on the lower floor of the office building. After they had sat down Brad launched into conversation.

"I didn't say anything on the way home from Julie's yesterday, but I want you to know that Julie and I are going to be married. I'd consider it an honor, John, if you would you be the best man."

"I had a hunch you and Julie would get married. Any real plans yet?"

"Not yet, except for deciding I'd like you to be my best man. I had thought about my younger brother, but you and I have been friends for a long time."

When the weekend rolled around Brad drove back to visit Julie. She met him at the front door with a hug and kiss, then led him to the sofa where they snuggled in to one another. Chrissy came bounding out of her room.

"Hi, Brad!" and bounced right back to her room.

"Julie, John said he'd be my best man."

"I thought about my sister for bridesmaid, but Carol is my best friend. Trouble is, she's still in Nashville. I'm not sure I should upset things down in Nashville by asking Carol to come back for our wedding. What do you think, Brad?"

Brad put his arm around Julie's shoulder.

"I'm inclined to agree with you, honey."

"I think I should ask my sister and write Carol to tell her why."

"Should we have a church wedding, Julie?"

"Oh, Brad. I'd like one, if we could. And I'd like Ben to accompany me down the aisle. I don't think my stepfather would mind."

"Julie, that's a great idea. Let's have Chrissy be flower girl. It will be wonderful!"

Since her divorce Julie had not been an active member of any particular church congregation. However, her mother and stepfather were members of a small church in town. She would go to the pastor of that church and ask if he would officiate at the wedding. Julie and Brad agreed on September 1 when the weather in Minnesota was still moderate. It would be a formal wedding. Julie wrote Carol to explain that she was marrying Brad because she truly loved him. She realized that the time he was gone to war gave her time to think that she had not loved and would not love anyone else.

Everything began to fall into place. Brad's parents and brother along with Julie's mother, stepfather, sister and friends attended a rehearsal dinner put on by Brad's parents at the local country club the night before the wedding. September 1 was a beautiful, balmy Saturday. The wedding had been scheduled for 10 a.m.

All eyes in the congregation watched Ben escort Julie down the aisle to stand beside Brad before the pastor. The pastor intoned the marriage ceremony as Brad and Julie faced each other. Just before that they had both walked over to the candle symbolic of a long life together and lit it.

John handed Brad the many diamond tiered wedding ring.

"Do you, Brad Owens, take Julie Evans to be your lawful wedded wife, to love and care for, in sickness and in health for the remainder of your life?"

"I will."

Julie felt as if she was in a dream. She heard the pastor asking her the same question and in a dreamy voice answered, "I will."

Brad slipped the wedding ring on Julie's finger.

"I now pronounce you man and wife. Brad, you may now kiss your bride."

Brad put his arm around Julie and kissed her sweetly and gently.

"Julie, I love you and always will."

"I love you too, Brad."

The congregation applauded. The pastor congratulated the couple.

They walked down the aisle to the back of the church. Julie had her arm through Brad's and smiled at each and every guest as they came through the reception line. They held a small reception in the basement of the church and then were whisked off in a limousine to a secret hideaway for a week-long honeymoon.

As Julie looked back through the window of the limo upon the group of family and friends waving good-bye from the church parking lot, she realized how very lucky she was. She had good friends, a wonderful family, and now, the man of her dreams. She knew that the future could be uncertain, but she knew, too, at this moment, that hers held nothing but promise.

# THE END